SWITCHING **TEAMS**

Dawn Elizabeth Waters

First published by Dog Ear Publishing
4011 Vincennes Rd
Indianapolis, IN 46268
www.dogearpublishing.net

ISBN: 978-1-4575-4307-4

This book is printed on acid-free paper.

Printed in the United States of America

To Yvette for making sense of the lyrics and loving me gently down the road until I arrived at the place where I could finally breathe. To my incredibly resilient and remarkable boys whose faces and love inspire me to be fearless every day. To all of the people who offered their wisdom, support and encouragement as this book experienced its own coming out process.

Table of Contents

PROLOGUE

The Game of Life

It's unbelievable how much you don't know about the game you have been playing all your life.

— *Mickey Mantle*

I magine how it would feel if you found yourself standing on the pitcher's mound warming up as you eagerly prepared to pitch the most important game of your career. It is the World Series and you are on whichever American League team happens to have emerged tops in the league. The sight of the hometown crowd standing on their feet and the sound of their cheers ringing in your ears is overwhelming and helps to pump you up for the task at hand. You have a role to play and expectations are very high. The game plan is to take one batter at a time and to throw your very best pitches depending on the situation. You analyze each batter and consider the ball and strike count.

Great teams are family to one another and have an unbreakable bond. Players have each other's backs no matter what. The pitcher is a lot like the captain of the ship when out on the field. If you stand on a pitcher's mound, you understand the pressure that comes with the position. You realize the importance of your role and take the job very seriously.

A baseball game is nine innings long. Your pitch count can range anywhere from twenty to over one hundred pitches. Sometimes the pitcher throws strikes and sometimes the batter puts one over the fence. Even the most amazing pitchers throw hanging curve balls every once in a while. When a batter sees one coming, it can change the landscape of the scoreboard if runners happen to be on base. Let's assume however that in this particular game the pitcher made all of the right decisions and pitched a solid game. The fourth inning rolls around and much to the surprise of everyone, the pitcher does not return to the mound. The fans are confused, the manager is angry, and, most of all, the pitcher is completely shocked by what is happening. Instead of heading back to the mound, the pitcher is informed there has been an immediate trade and is handed the opposing team's uniform to change into. The job is now to go out and pitch against the team he had been on just moments ago.

The reaction of the fans is incredulous. The randomness of the turn in events puzzles everyone, including the pitcher. Some view it as a betrayal, others as an opportunity for success. The overall reaction greatly depends on which side of the stadium you sit or where your loyalties fall. If you are that pitcher, there is no other option for you. The decision has been made and if you want to continue to do what you love doing and what you feel is right, you have to do what you have to do. The only options are to fight it or accept it. The game has changed. Often when life changes, it is sudden and unexpected. The only constant in life is change. You have to wrap your brain around the fact you are wearing a brand new, unfamiliar uniform and you still have to move forward. It is difficult to hear the criticism and the echoes of anger unleashed on you not only as an athlete, but as a person.

You are exactly the same person that got up in the morning. The only change is found in the perception of those who witnessed this turn of events. Loyalties immediately shifted, opinions changed, and judgments formed based on the new situation. In the blink of an eye, everything changed for everyone. This is where my story begins.

DAWN ELIZABETH WATERS

I suspect for those who may not be sports enthusiasts this analogy may require some additional clarification. I am the pitcher. The innings in the baseball game correspond to the decades of my life. Everything changed in the fourth inning of my life. No tragedy befell me, no one died, but life as I knew it was completely turned upside down. My very comfortable existence as someone's wife and stay at home mother of three was gone the instant I came out as a lesbian. Since that day, everything changed for me. Coming out has been both liberating and devastating, and it easily tops the list of challenges I have faced in forty years of walking upon the earth. When I piece together all the movie clips from my journey up to this point, I realized I have been living an inauthentic life.

It has been difficult trying to keep up with all of the changes that have come my way. You name it, it changed. I tried my best to wade through it all gracefully, but some days this was not the case. I was as graceful as a linebacker in a ballet recital. I found little help as I searched for guidance on navigating life after such a huge change. I knew right out of the gate no manual existed that covered what I was going through. This was of little comfort on some of those especially tough days early on. I just wanted someone to tell me exactly what to do to move forward.

In a nutshell, I am a lesbian, divorced, Christian woman who is a registered independent. I am pro-choice and do not believe in the death penalty. I am a mother of three boys, a small business owner, and a feminist. I understand if you need a moment to wrap your brain around that sentence because at times my brain cramps when I think about it. I am a Realtor and co-owner of an event photography business. In addition to this, I have also been a certified personal trainer who has worked with clients who are as successful as they have chosen to be. My philosophy when working with these clients mirrored my own personal philosophy about life. It is quite simple. Discipline, faith, determination, and a positive mindset are the keys to healthy living. Be fearless. Seek truth, even if it hurts, and above all else love without hesitation. As we think, so shall we be. Staying grounded in this philosophy was difficult when I was faced with my new reality as a lesbian.

My revelation did not come in a flash or in an instant. It happened over the course of many years but built real steam after I married and began a family. I had made it my mission to figure out what in me was wrong and to get to the bottom of it so my children could have the most put together mother possible. Everything felt like a struggle for a long time. I woke up each day and fought just to hold things together. I could not eat or sleep well for many years. The anxiety I had running rampant in me was suffocating.

I was in a continual search for relief and never expected that discovering I was gay would be the deep cleansing breath that had eluded me for so long. I was elated to feel air flowing freely from my chest, but I understood the world as I knew it was about to change. Figuring out my new place looked a lot like a blacksmith attempting to forge a sword out of sand. I was instantly forced to step out of the familiar confines of my life and readjust. The majority of my adult life took place along the beaten path. Now, I live on the road less traveled. This road is unpaved, riddled with potholes, and full of twists and turns. This road is lined with those who are ready to define their lives and their surroundings based on their own terms.

There was not one specific moment when the light bulb went off. I was vaguely aware something was not right within me. I spent many years trying to figure out if this deep seated intangible flaw was the result of nature or nurture. I was on a mission to find inner peace and joy. I picked up the shovel and began to dig out of the ditch of emotional and mental crud surrounding me. As the years went on, I evaluated every little facet of my life with a microscope.

As I searched for the answers to the questions I pondered about life and finding peace, I discovered concepts and truths that stuck with me as I looked for answers and clarity. I examined every inch of my life, including my childhood, my marriage, my parenting, my friendships, and my personality. I never considered my sexuality should have been included in that very long list.

I have been asked many times, by many people, how I knew I was a lesbian. I have been asked when I knew, have I always known, or was this something that just hit me on the head like a brick. How could I have been married and have had only experiences with men my whole life and now discover I was gay? There are no short answers to these questions. It makes no sense. What I know is that I felt so relieved when I figured it out. I felt free. For the first time in my life. I felt comfortable in my earth suit.

When I came to a place of self-acceptance, my world opened up. I realized while my circumstances had changed, the fundamental core of who I was had not. I discovered a new found freedom within my mind, body, and spirit that finally allowed me to share my true self with the world.

Sharing my journey with those who can relate to what I have gone through is only one reason why I wrote this book. My audience also includes those who may not "get" the gay thing as well as any person who has dealt with change in their lives. I hope by offering a glimpse into my experience someone else may see the joy that living an authentic life can bring.

The premise of switching sides is one we can all relate to in some way or another. As I share my journey, I offer two suggestions. First, keep an open mind as you read. Second, resist the temptation to judge my experience or my stand on certain issues. I believe sharing what I have gone through will offer encouragement and reinforce the idea that collectively our similarities far outweigh our differences.

My unique situation includes views from both sides of the field. One of the most amazing qualities of the human spirit is the ability to view things from many sides and to then decide what works. We all have perceptions that cloud our willingness to listen to those who do not agree with our positions. Adjusting to life as a lesbian has not been easy, but life is not easy. There is no greater gift we give ourselves than to be authentic and stand in truth regardless of what the world may think.

I want anyone who chooses to share in my experience to realize that it is just that — my experience. I am not trying to win over anyone or present a case for anything in particular. In my life I have found shared experiences and feelings can unite us even if there are differences in our worldview. I firmly believe it is better to be kind than right. Open minds are the foundation on which peace can be constructed. My hope is that this book helps and touches people – that someone reading it might realize they are not alone and that they, too, have the ability to embrace change and be fearless. I pray those who have strong opinions about my homosexuality will be able to see past my sexual orientation and see a picture of what it is like to be human.

DAWN ELIZABETH WATERS

CHAPTER 1

The Road to Truth

*The truth will set you free,
but first it will make you miserable.*

— *James Garfield*

I never imagined at the age of forty I would be divorced, raising three children, living in a rental house, and embracing life as a lesbian. Thankfully, I was born with a pretty good sense of humor which helped make the adjustment slightly more bearable. I have been told my penchant for bathroom humor and quick wit is one of the many genes inherited from my father's side of the family. That is how my mother told it, anyway. Comedy has lightened many situations, lifted me from dark times, and served as a constant when everything seemed shaky.

It is safe to say my version of humor was met with a less than enthusiastic reaction when I was younger. The adults in my life, mainly my parents, were not always appreciative of my comments or quips. I had earned the reputation of a smart mouthed girl who enjoyed stirring the pot and had a fondness for engaging in tough girl activities. I am fairly certain my memory of being referred to lovingly as "Dawn the Demon" was both well-deserved and supported by fact.

I had my own unique perspective as a child which usually went against the current of mainstream thinking. I was the salmon swimming up the stream most of the time. I could not help myself. I pushed limits and played devil's advocate. I had a mouth on me and, for better or worse, was never shy inserting it into any discussion. I was the kid who always asked why and was never content to accept things just because they were. If I was told no, I wanted an explanation. If I felt the explanation was not adequate, I would continue to question the issue at hand. How did the priest turn the wafer into Jesus? Why can't women play professional baseball? I have a new appreciation for what raising a child like this is all about because I was blessed with a child just like me. Sorry Mom and Dad.

I was a shit stirrer most of my life. Sometimes it had a purpose and other times I did it just for sport. I had a fat lip for most of my teen years, which I blame on my poor sense of timing, improper delivery, and my choice of inappropriate tone. I was sarcastic and often negative. Much later I recognized that this was a defense mechanism that helped mask what was going on under the surface.

This is the part of the book where I go back and shake loose the dust from the curtains of my childhood. While the past is the past and cannot be altered, reflecting on it played an important role in my healing and acceptance of who I was. In my mind, my life is divided into four distinct categories: little Dawn, teen Dawn, adult Dawn, and the real Dawn.

I am the oldest of three children. I was a tomboy and on most days in my youth I looked like I had never seen a hairbrush or even a mirror. Girly things did not matter to me, much to the dismay of my mom. She tried for years to get me to wear dresses and to stop playing with trucks and Matchbox cars in mud puddles. On the days she did manage to get me in something more fitting of a young lady, I would inevitably ruin it by climbing a tree or sliding on the grass while playing tackle football. It was a losing battle. I did have Barbie dolls but I was more interested in super heroes or Star Wars.

My dad worked and my mom stayed at home. My dad and I have always been close. Each year on my birthday, he calls and makes a point of sharing that he remembers the day I was born like it was yesterday. My mom was the room mother for my school for many years and was always at there when I returned from school each day. We always had a comfortable home, food to eat, and clean clothes. I was not beaten up on a regular basis. How could I say that my childhood was unhappy when I was provided the physical necessities? I did not have the messed up childhood that some kids have. I always thought of people who had it a lot worse than I did and felt like it was inappropriate for me to complain. It was not that big of a deal, right? My blinding light bulb moment came when the therapist told me what made it a big deal was how I felt about it.

I was my parents' first born child and from photos I can tell you Little Dawn was really cute. My dad was a professional baseball player and when he and my mom married they were often on the road together. They lived the ball player's life. Sleeping late, ball games, and late night partying was the norm. They toted me along with them. My mom made every attempt to shield me from any danger, germ, or potentially hazardous situation. I was the textbook overprotected first child. My head was always covered to prevent infections, I was always on a blanket when on the floor which acted a barrier to any possible contamination, and was hovered over. My mother's goal was to keep me safe, healthy, and in her sight. As a mom, I can understand this way of thinking. Infants need this type of care. My mother's approach, however, followed me well into my teenage years.

Growing up, I was afraid of many things. When I was in elementary school, I was convinced that when I returned from school each day my family would all be dead. I constantly created worse case scenarios in my mind. I could not help it. Dad coming home later than usual meant that he was in an accident. You get the idea. This was not exactly taken seriously. I was laughed at and told I was being ridiculous, which did not help. While this seemed completely irrational to everyone else, the fear was real for me. I remember feeling unsettled from a very young age.

The fact that my earliest memory is of splitting my tongue open and needing stitches sheds a little light on what was running through my little Dawn brain at the age of 3. The story of that day is legendary in my family because I was hard to treat once we got to the emergency room. I still vividly recall what the bloody wash cloth in my mouth looked and tasted like and the scenery out the backseat window as we sped to the hospital. I remember the green room I was put in and refusing to open my mouth. Eventually they had to knock me out to put the stitches in. When it came time to take the stitches out, I bit through the tongue depressors and fought the entire time. The doctor gave up and they just came out on their own. This is one hell of a first memory to have.

There were many years I never cried. I jokingly identified with the Tin Man from the Wizard of Oz, only it was not a joke. The Tin Man's lack of a heart and cold metal exterior was something I related to. I did the best I could to maintain exterior protection around me at all times. These were my walls. The irony was that while I had a very hard time letting myself cry I had absolutely no problem letting my anger fly or my temper flare. I found myself in the habitual cycle of blowing up and feeling bad shortly thereafter as I recognized what I did was wrong, and then wanting to change what I had done. The next time someone pushed my buttons, however, I would do the same thing. I knew when let I my emotions get the best of me the result would not be productive in any way. Yet I still continued reacting. I simply did not know where to put my frustration with the world during those teen years. There is no more confounding creature on earth than a teenager. You know this is true.

I operated primarily out of anger for many years. Being angry helped fortify the protective walls I constructed around me. When I was little, my mom feared something would happen to me. In response to that fear, I was kept on a short leash. She preferred my friends coming to our house and as

I got older my requests for freedom were frequently denied. Controlling where I went and what I did was her way of keeping me safe and helping lessen the fear controlling her. I was angry because of the inconsistent reactions my mom had to everyday events. I felt like I had no power in that environment, which contributed to my developing anxiety and many insecurities.

I believed at the time these traits were central to who I was, could never be changed, and were something I would have to deal with for the rest of my life. As I left for college my anger went with me. I was on my own for the first time and took full advantage of my freedom and had the grades to prove it. The first two years were rough and there came a point in time when it was clear counseling was the only way I would be able to get my finger off of the self-destruct button. Thankfully, through therapy, I learned that surface emotions were like the skin covering a piece of fruit. To get to the fruit I had to deal with the underlying issues in order to be healthy. While becoming aware of the impact that growing up in an overprotective environment where alcohol addiction was present did help me begin to heal, it did not completely rid me of my anxiety. Little victories. As my time in therapy came to an end, I was hired by the intramural sports coordinator to be the assistant coordinator for the women's intramural program at the university. From the time we met, we worked well as a team. In fact, we worked so well together we decided to get married.

The Diamond

In 20 years together, we had want and we had plenty. He was my best friend and our marriage reflected it. Our friendship was the core of our relationship, the rest was just gravy. We had each other and that was all we needed. He proposed to me on the third base line of my high school baseball field on his birthday in 1993. We were excited for our future and were married at a state park in April of 1994. Almost immediately, we embarked on the first job related move of many in the first few years of our married life. I had just graduated college and he had just received his master's degree when we married. We were young and ready to take on the world. He was my guy. We had plans for our future and always managed to have what we needed to survive those early days of dating and marriage. We lived in apartments, ate spaghetti and ravioli from a can, and many times had $5 left in our bank account after our bills were paid. We racked up crushing credit card debt but were fortunate enough to have had the opportunity to pull ourselves out of it. We always felt so blessed and made it a priority to learn from each mistake we knew we would make along our way.

In those early days, each move took a toll on me and fed my constant anxiety. I am certain he sometimes wished I was different and would figure out how to get over my anxiousness. I knew the burden of my issues was something we both carried yet he never complained or pushed me to get over the crap that just seemed to never disappear. I was sick of my own self so I can imagine how he must have felt about it all. In one of the wedding cards we received was a prayer that really made a very powerful impact on us both. We kept this card and I looked at it more times than I can count over the years. It was a reminder to us that marriage was not easy and it would take living these words in order to have a happy and healthy one. I know being mindful of these words helped play a huge role in how we both chose to go forward after I dropped the gay bomb on our lives.

The prayer reads:

> *Keep us O Lord, from pettiness. Let us be thoughtful in word and deed. Help us put away pretense, and face each other in deep trust without fear or self-pity. Help us to guard against fault-finding, and be quick to discover the best in each other and in every situation. Guard us from ill temper and hasty judgment; encourage us to take time for all things, to grow calm, serene and gentle. Help us to be generous with*

kind words and compliments. Teach us never to ignore, never to hurt, and never to take each other for granted. Engrave charity and compassion on our hearts.

We began our family and survived a life or death scare with our second son when he was an infant. We took turns falling apart sitting at the bedside of our little fighter. My second son was born on a beautiful March morning after a surprisingly quick labor and delivery. Our first son was a 28 hour marathon labor and I was thrilled this one took three hours from induction to delivery. I remember the instant they handed him to me after he was delivered. I did not experience the initial flood of elation I had had with my first son, but rather a feeling that something was not right. My first words were "Is he okay?" Everyone assured me he was fine but there was something amiss as far as I was concerned. Moms just know. I had a sense something was off. I could not figure out why my gut was so unsettled in those first moments of his life. My gut was right. He was born with a severe heart defect and at three months of age almost died. He was hospitalized for 6 weeks while doctors did everything they could to get him well.

My husband and I took turns falling apart while the other remained strong. We were there in ways only we could be for one another. I watched my husband sobbing at his side when the specialist informed us we needed to be prepared for him to be put on the transplant list. We both sat up for two nights straight in his room listening to the ventilator help him breath while suffering through the constant sound of machines beeping. For the next six weeks, I called the hospital home. There were times in those first few days I began to prepare for the possibility of losing him. I remember thinking at one point it would be alright if he died because I hadn't felt like I had bonded with him and had not fully attached to him because he'd only been with us for three months. This thought haunted me for years. I was riddled with guilt and questioned what kind of a mother would think that. I later realized it was my way of preparing for the worst and a stage of my own unique grief over the situation.

Events like this have been known to rip families and marriages apart. We escaped that. We had our inside jokes and private humor. We had fun no matter what we were doing. This marriage was not supposed to end, ever. When we made our wedding promises under the giant, old live oak tree at the state park, we meant every word. We were mindful of the reading from Corinthians that was part of our ceremony and tried to remain true to it every day from that moment forward.

Our journey together was uniquely ours and we cherished it to the point of bragging at times. Our identity was very much tied to us as a couple. We had great parties and were a great team all the way around. Whether it was parenting, teaching classes at church together, knocking out a room that needed painting, or working in the yard, there was no team more efficient than we were. We could juggle a crazy schedule with a hundred events and manage to get all the kids where they needed to be without a hitch. On those crazy days, we would land side by side on the couch and just be. We were that good together. Even so, this could not change the fact that life as we knew it was going to be altered and our marriage of almost 17 years was going to end.

Of course, the marriage was not without its bumps. There were communication issues I had always attributed to the differences between men and women. I often felt like I was the weak link. He was a very easy going and a relatively unshakable kind of guy. When life would get bumpy, it never seemed to rattle him. He would roll with changes, look forward to unexpected adventures, and was a pretty happy guy in general. His patience was something I always was truly thankful for. I was certain I was the one who brought the majority of baggage into our relationship. I had the issues. I worked and struggled long and hard to get to the core of them so I could be a healthy part of the team we had created. He was the type of person I wished I could be.

If I had to choose only one word to describe my marriage and relationship with him, the word would be kind. We were always kind to one another. We had a deeply forged commitment to one another born out of love. We chose to deal with each other gently and with compassion and kindness. We actually didn't find this to be much of a challenge. I cannot explain why it seemed so easy to be married when so many others around us struggled with their relationships and marriages, but we never took it for granted. It was just us. Even in our moments of frustration with one another, we never got nasty or took shots at each other. That type of behavior always seemed so unproductive. We both were problem solvers which was very helpful when we had to resolve conflicts or disagreements.

I reviewed my life and saw I had a very kind husband, three relatively pleasant children, and a very nice material life. I really wanted for nothing. My marriage was not a train wreck — it was actually quite the opposite — which made it that much more difficult to entertain the idea I was gay. When I acknowledged this inkling within me, everything changed. My anxiety was on the rise and I just could not believe the fact that this was a possibility. I suffered many sleepless nights and tried like hell to settle myself down, to regroup, and to once again begin the search for the one last rock I kept missing. This elusive rock would prove to be a boulder that was rolling down the mountain I was trying to climb.

Historically, I never had a problem with homosexuality, but most of my life I had a gigantic complex about being seen as gay. I would ask my husband or friends if I looked too "butchy" after getting dressed. I had no idea where this constant question came from. It would nag my brain and I would need reassurance I looked okay. I never felt right in my skin. I was teased for not developing right along with the other girls in my grade so I attributed my insecurities about how I looked to that. How I thought I looked and how I was feeling about myself clashed because I felt very out of place most of the time. My self-esteem was at its peak when I was playing sports. I fit there. There was no expectation of make up or dresses or even brushed hair.

I did not look out of place with catcher's gear on behind home plate or on a volleyball or basketball court. I was at home and felt amazing when I was doing what I loved. I hid behind my jock persona for a very long time and it worked for me.

The Real Truth

For many years, I was the head coach for the "something must be wrong with me" team. This thought floated across my mind for as long as I can remember. I figured the lack of comfort in my own skin was due to one of two things. First were the circumstances in my life beyond my control, namely my lingering childhood issues. Second was the result of every apparent character flaw I saw when I looked in the mirror. In the search for my authentic self, I had to do whatever I could to get to the real me. This meant digging up the dirt, chasing the ghosts of my past, and getting to know who I really was. This also meant turning over each of the rocks lining the path of my life and taking a very close look at everything. The end result of this process was life changing.

I believed I had found the answers I needed and the magical door of normal would soon appear. I had done the work by spending many years meticulously scraping the hardened clay from the bottom of my cleats. Every time I thought I finally figured out what to do with all of the things that had happened in my life, I would feel relieved for a short time. Yet something still was not quite right. There was a nagging anxiety I could not kick. I wondered what else there could there be? I had been searching for so long for the one thing that would offer relief from the anxiety threatening my life. Once I recognized my sexual orientation played a part in my struggle, I had the courage to begin a journey I knew would be difficult not only for myself, but everyone in my life. I found myself reviewing the video of my life and saw clues which supported my new reality. I wondered how I missed the many signs pointing to the possibility of my being a lesbian.

My favorite verse from the bible expresses this in blunt terms. "Then you will know the truth, and the truth will set you free" (John 8:32). Searching for one's truth is what living authentically means. For me, searching for my truth stripped away the victim suit I frequently wore and brought humility and an awareness of how my actions affected others. Becoming authentic required an acceptance of the fact I was wonderfully made despite how I felt about myself on any given day. It meant accepting my worth and value was not based on anything I said or did or any role I played. In one moment of authenticity, I had to face that life as I knew it would drastically be altered. The scene of my truth setting me free looked like giant waves crashing on the beach during a storm, yet at my core was peace.

Once I came out, I found myself staring at the completely new and slightly terrifying reality of starting over. Authenticity is defined as the quality or condition of being authentic, trustworthy or genuine. As everything unraveled, the only way I could make sense of what was happening around me was to remain focused on my desire to be authentic.

My single goal was to leave as little debris in my wake as possible. Change is hard and going through significant changes can be a lonely process. I thought at times I had the granddaddy of all change happening to me. I spent many moments in my own head. My truth was painful for my family and I carried the burden of guilt for every bit of it. This guilt crippled me emotionally for a very long time. I resented being different. I resented being the cause of their pain and having to deal with a new normal, and I was angry, again.

CHAPTER 2

Curve Ball

Only do what your heart tells you.

—*Princess Diana*

Discovering I am gay was a shock. Discovering I was in love with my best friend was even more shocking. My family would not be the only casualty of this war raging within myself. Her family would also suffer and the impact of this unexpected turn of events would be exponential.

The first person I came out to was my best friend of ten years, who also happened to be the love of my life. We both knew this was how it was supposed to be and knew we could not ignore these feelings or revelations any longer. This was going to be the talk of the town for sure. The headlines in the local news may have read something like this, "Two very involved women from the Catholic church lost their minds, turned their backs on their families, and were in the midst of a full on midlife crisis as they threw away their lives and became lesbians." Our story was a private one, full of love and joy. There was a high probability, however, that as far as the world was concerned the story and the facts would never be accepted.

Coming out did not just affect me. There were eight people between two families who had to sort through the broken pieces of what life was supposed to look like. When glass shatters it flies everywhere. When glass breaks it can take a long time to get every single remnant cleaned up. Cleaning up broken glass is the worst. You can think you have it all, only to discover tiny shards days, weeks, even months later. Our families would be cleaning up for a very long time. I was aware of the mess that coming out would create yet I was undeterred from what I had to do. I knew part of my journey would be to tell my best friend I was in love with her.

My best friend and I were as close as they come. We met in 2001 when our oldest children were four. I knew from our first meeting that mornings were not her favorite time of the day. I entered a room and saw an obviously unhappy woman standing at a copy machine. "Good morning already, huh?" were the first words I spoke to her. She responded with a grunt and possibly even an eye roll as she continued to mope over the copies she was frantically trying to complete. I thought it was funny. For the rest of the day, I made it my mission to get this miserable lady to smile. As the morning wore on, we had an actual conversation and commiserated about what a pain working at vacation bible school was. I was assigned to T-shirt painting and she was assisting the director of religious education, also known as her mom.

We took to each other very quickly and became very close. We had kids the same age and had very similar interests. Our personalities meshed from the start. When we first met, I was struggling with many things and she seemed to be in the same emotional place I was. We bonded over muddling through motherhood, dealing with toddlers, and the stay-at-home mother lifestyle.

It was the healthiest and easiest friendship I'd ever had as an adult. We spent a lot of time together hashing out our demons and just trying to survive motherhood on a daily basis. Our friendship was equal parts brutal honesty and compassionate understanding. We bent each other's ears about everything. We celebrated mini personal victories and shared in one another's most desperate times. Our friendship was one that was rare. I felt her victories and shared in her defeats, whether self-inflicted or otherwise.

Raising children and dealing with life was much easier with her on the other end of the phone. Our families grew very close and we always managed to have fun regardless of what was going on in the periphery. We hoped our oldest children would become fast friends and when they didn't, we decided to still be friends anyway. Our individual lives became intertwined. I had relationships with friends prior to her that were close in nature, but my relationship with her was a blessing unlike any other I found.

The thing I loved the most about her was her heart. She was happiest when things were going well for me. The genuine joy she expressed when I was doing well and making great strides in my own life was a beautiful gift. I have never met a person with a more loving and caring heart than she possessed. I learned many lessons from her about being a better mom, person, and friend. I learned how to be a more patient caretaker when my kids were sick by watching how patient and gentle she was when her son was sick. Her world stopped so that she could be there right next to him for whatever he needed. She was a selfless person who put her own needs or wishes below those of the people around her.

In addition to the countless animals she has rescued from traffic, and the gallons of blood she has donated in her lifetime, she donated bone marrow to a complete stranger a few years after we met. A little girl in England was saved because of her generosity. There was nothing she would not do for someone else. I felt honored to call her friend. I remember not asking her for much because I liked doing things on my own and was not one to ask for help in anything. I used to frustrate the hell out of her because of my stubbornness when it came to needing help. I was the helper, the one to come in and rescue people from all kinds of things. We built a relationship over many years and at some point I remember feeling like we were too close. I wanted to tell her things first. I found I was disappointed when we had plans to go somewhere and they did not materialize. I always liked being in her company whether it was in person or on the phone.

We would go on an annual beach get-away with two of our close friends. These weekends were nothing spectacular and usually were spent in pajamas eating chips, chocolate, and drinking "big girl" beverages. We'd stay up late, sleep in, and spend our days roaming the beach and watching our favorite movies. It was our time to get away, to be able to breathe and think about whatever the household drama of the week was. We all took turns sharing whatever was happening in our lives and left the weekend feeling recharged. I hated packing up to go back home from these weekends. Life seemed so much simpler while at the beach. Thoughts seemed clearer and there were not any problems that couldn't be solved within the confines of these trips. We always thought there was nothing better for the soul than sand pedicures and breathing in the ocean air. There are few things that rival a weekend away at the beach with your girlfriends. There was such power, grace, and love squeezed into those few short days.

When I was away on my first, and last, week long cruise to the Eastern Caribbean, she helped me survive my in-laws and the 13 to 20 foot seas with her instant messages. On the ship, I felt cut off from civilization and not being able to speak to her or any of my other friends was not fun. That week ranks high on the list of longest weeks in my life. Number one being the week after I told my husband I was gay. When I returned, she was my first call. I had survived and wanted to see everyone that night to recap and tell all of my crazy cruise stories.

I talked her through her classes as she went back to school to get her degree in photography. I shared her surprise when she found out she was pregnant, gave her all of my best tricks to stave off morning sickness, and drove her to the doctor when she miscarried. This heartbreak was something we both felt deeply. We truly shared everything. These things brought us closer every time.

We vacationed as couples a few months after she had the miscarriage. On this trip, we were able to take leave of our daily responsibilities to the kids and be freer than we would have been at home. She and I found ourselves up past when our husbands had gone to bed most nights. One particular memory I have of this trip happened after a night of drinking liter sized bottles of margaritas. In our inebriated state, we decided we were going to take a walk around the resort. I am sure any who saw us that night would describe it more as a late night stumble. Next I knew we were looking at some fish in a fish tank and in my drunken state I thought it would be funny to ask her a random question. "What would you do if I kissed you right now?" She turned toward me, punched me in the arm and said "Get the fuck outta here."

Of course I laughed, because I was joking. Wasn't I? I was laughing but I was mortified those words had come from my mouth. What the hell was wrong with me? Nothing ever happened that night or any other night. To this day I am not sure what I would have done had she answered my question any other way than she did. After we returned, she supported me as I began preparing myself for my son's open heart surgery, which was scheduled for the following month. She let me be as I spent most of the weeks prior to the surgery lying in my bed watching television in order to cope with it all. She kept an eye on me, knowing I needed to do what I needed to do to prepare for this unpleasant family event. She made me get in the car to drive to the hospital when I did not think I could get in. She talked me off of the ledge when I was at the hospital as my son underwent a heart catheter procedure and the open heart surgery. She listened as I ranted about how eight year olds should not have to endure such pain and how terrified I was about how this experience might affect my boy afterwards. She listened as I wept, sobbed, and yelled about how much this whole thing sucked. These were the things we did for one another. We were just as willing and ready to be there for the little things as we were for the big, giant things.

I watched her graduate with honors from photography school and remember feeling deep down I had never been more proud of her than I was at that moment. We started a photography business together and decided we were going to kick some ass doing what we loved to do. There was nothing the two of us could not accomplish. We had the support of our friends and our spouses and the world seemed right, except something was wrong. During the last couple of years before I confessed my feelings to her, there was a tension we were both feeling. Nothing tragic had happened that would have caused a strain on the friendship. It was just a feeling. The strange thing was that, as close as we were all those years, I had never shared with her the feelings I was developing towards her. I was completely convinced I had lost my mind.

It is still unbelievable that neither one of us said a word to the other about the strange emotions that were rolling around in both of our heads. Never. There are many who had a hard time believing we never shared how we were feeling about one another given that we had been friends for so long. There would be times I would not hear from her for a few days and get worried I had done something to piss her off. She would take her camera and head to the beach, taking photos to try to work through how she was feeling with regard to me. I had no idea what was going on. She was a vault and would never tell me what was really going on. I always assumed her solitary trips to the beach had more to do with the struggles she was having in her marriage. I came to find out she too was thinking and feeling the exact same thing about me and about herself.

Much later she showed me the images she had taken while out on one mental health day. The photos were beautifully dark and sad. They became some of my favorite images because they were a visual representation of how we were both feeling unbeknownst to each other. I cherish these images and each time I look at them I am reminded about how difficult this journey has been for both of us in our own ways. We were experiencing our own processes without the other one knowing what was going on.

Our 10 year friendship played an important part in how I came to know I was gay. The rationalizations ran rampant in my brain. "You're friends and of course you feel things for her, that's what friends do. She is your best friend, there is just something wrong with you, Dawn." I even put stock in the fact that women are emotional creatures and are able to share deeper connections with one another. My thoughts ran back and forth. "This is perfectly normal. This is crazy." For whatever reason, it was through this friendship I was finally able to conclude that what was rolling through my mind was not insanity. I knew for sure about four months before I decided to take that fearless leap of faith and step into my authentic self. My suspicions about my sexuality were confirmed long before I spoke a word to her. I had no idea what I was going to do about it, but I knew without question it was the truth. I knew what this could mean and do to my family and I tried like hell to make it not be the case.

The Last Piece

My biggest project over the past few years had been to actualize my authentic self. I was determined not to allow any more bullshit and to find out what I was really all about — what I believed, who I was, and who I wasn't. I had decided to press forward toward who I was meant to be. When your kids get older, you realize there is more to who you are than the things you do. I am not sure why this seems to occur around the age of 40, but it did for me.

An opportunity to participate in a fearless living retreat out on the west coast came my way as I was wrestling with how I felt about her. I spent hours completing the long application and contemplated whether or not I would have a chance at being chosen for one of the six spots available for the "Starting Over Intensive Program." The retreat was going to be hosted and facilitated by Rhonda Britten at her home in California. She is the founder of the Fearless Living Institute and was a host for a television show I used to watch called *Starting Over*. This Emmy award winning reality show focused on the lives of six women who lived in the Starting Over house. The premise was to encourage the women to make changes and deal with the recurring issues hindering their growth. I watched because I could relate to the struggles they were having and hoped to steal some helpful tips about how to get past my own obstacles.

All of the women came from diverse backgrounds and brought quite a bit of personal baggage into the house with them. The goal was to face their fears. Through individual life coaching, group activities, and personal challenges, they learned how to go forward with new eyes and a new mind-set. There were no issues too big or too small to tackle. They were frightened women who were abused and neglected; they struggled with self-esteem, weight, financial issues, anxiety, depression, and addictions. I was a huge fan of the program. Many times I saw something that helped me recognize something in my life that needed addressing.

It took a few days to compile the application and when it was done I faxed it off without any hesitation. I could envision going to California for five days to see if the experience would help me finally get past my lingering, nameless funk which persisted despite my best efforts to get rid of it through therapy, hypnosis, prayer, and my vast library of self-help books. The fact that I could see myself taking a long trip alone to somewhere new was proof I had made great progress in my fight against anxiety and fear. The years of therapy and the expansion of my self-improvement library had helped me arrive at a much healthier place. I was proud of myself. When word came that I was accepted for the weekend, I panicked. While I was thrilled to have been chosen, it made me think I must be pretty bad off in order to have been chosen so quickly. I must have set off all of the "this girl is a wreck" alarms with my responses. I thought participating in this retreat would finally allow me to get to the root of my problems and that the cost involved would be money well spent. I was ready to kick off the last bits of clay from my cleats and face whatever I had to. Before I could accept the invitation, I had a moment of fear and reality hit me like a ton of bricks. I knew what I knew in that instant.

I could no longer excuse away how I was feeling. I could no longer ignore what I knew was the truth. I knew I was in fact gay and I knew if I went to this weekend this news would surely have to be shared. This was the final piece of my puzzle. I sent word via email I was withdrawing my application along with my thanks for the opportunity to attend. My husband and best friend were confused as to why I decided not to go ahead with this trip. I could not tell anyone the reason I had changed my mind. I am sure I made up excuses about the money or the timing or something along those lines which would have not caused anyone to question me. The simple act of filling out the application gave me the clarity to put down on paper what was in my heart. My responses were free from the influence of any outside opinions, rationalizations, and, more importantly, fear. I still have a copy of the application tucked away I look at on occasion when I feel fear creeping in.

As I sat, I was immediately gripped by fear, disbelief, and a sense of dread. Anyway this went, it would be shocking and would have an impact of far reaching proportions. Rearranging the lineup of my life after 39 years would not be fair to everyone else.

I had two choices. The first was to sit on this, live the life I had freely chosen, and make peace with the fact that I made my bed and I had to lie in it. That choice made my heart sink so low I swear I would feel it hitting the cold hard cement beneath me. The other choice I had was to come clean and to let my truth be known. I could choose to stand up and let the chips fall where they may. This was about my life and my life was important. I finally had the guts to be truly authentic. I was not sure in those early days if I possessed the strength and resolve necessary to take on whatever would come at me because of my new orientation. I ignored the doubts rolling around and could hear myself yelling for the first time ever that this was important and it had to be done.

It took me another few months to get up the courage and to pick the right time to share this with her. I would vacillate between courageous and cowardly during that time. I fought against the knowledge that the familiar was very comfortable even if it bred self-contempt. My authentic self was in a full on battle with my practical and peace loving side. This was a huge risk and I was unsure I would be willing to take it given all that was at stake. I tried my best to come up with viable solutions to this dilemma so I would not have to choose one thing over the other. Could I have both? What would that look like? If I could have found a way to make this square peg fit into the round hole, I would have chosen that without fail. No matter what angle I examined, the lines did not match up.

I retreated into myself and began a phase of my life that had the strangest feel. I felt disconnected from things and spent many days just going through the motions of whatever the day brought. I was present but not awake. I began to consider how I was going to share this with her. I had a sneaking suspicion maybe she was having some feelings of her own regarding me. There was a growing, tangible tension when we were together. There was a weird vibe happening between us.

I am known for my mix CD's over the years among my group of friends. I love randomly surfing iTunes to find silly and interesting music. I make them for any occasion. I have mixes filled with angry music, ones that are very spiritual, some decade themed, and others of just favorite songs in my collection. I went back and perused the collections I had made for her over the years. To my surprise, many of them contained songs I referred to only as "songs I like." I did not know it at the time, but they were, in essence, love songs. I shared these with her long before I even knew they were about her.

We went to Miami to photograph an event about a month prior to my telling her. I had every intention of discussing my feelings with her on that trip, but the timing did not seem right. We worked long days at an airshow with thousands of people and we both needed to be on our game. My feelings would be a big newsflash and I did not want to mess up the work we were doing by dropping this bomb. I always seemed to find a reason to delay this conversation.

When I finally told her, I was completely ready to move forward with my realization whether she felt the same way or not. I was prepared for any response although I secretly hoped the feelings were mutual. A few days before I told her, I remember asking her if she ever had anything she could not tell anyone. She was puzzled by this and wondered quietly to herself what I might be referring to since I customarily told her everything. She did not ask questions or press me for more information, which was completely unlike her. The night I finally picked up the phone to tell her was very chilly. It was Christmas day and very late at night. We had not spoken that day and I was wondering why I had not heard from her. I came to find out she was giving me "a break from her crap" as she put it. As I made the call, I decided to censor nothing and say it all out loud. I needed to rip off the Band-Aid so I could move forward.

I said I had something I needed to tell her and I did not know where to start. I think I began rambling on about how people have feelings and how sometimes these feelings are confusing. I stumbled over every word, thought, and sentence from that point on and began talking in what sounded like gibberish in my own head. I think she actually was the one who finished my sentence and let me off the hook.

To this day, she laughs about how I, the one with all the words, completely lost the ability to form a coherent sentence that night. We both confessed to having these feelings and then boldly declared almost at the same time, "Well, we can't do anything about it." That statement was the topic of the rest of the conversation.

Even so, we were both relieved to find our independent feelings for one another were reciprocated and neither one of us was crazy. It was a personal victory for both of us that evening to be freed from the mental straightjackets we'd been wearing. We spoke at length about how we had never felt this way before about any other person, let alone a woman. Now keep in mind, neither one of us had any experience with a woman sexually.

We had no frame of reference. We were treading on grounds never explored before. We had a difficult time labeling just what this was during that first conversation. Were we gay? Were we bi? Were we just in love with each other? Whichever it was, we were sure life as we both knew it would never be the same as before. We wondered if things like this really happened outside of the movies. If it did, we had never heard of it before, let alone known of anyone who this had happened to. We knew no matter how this played out, it was going to be big.

When I hung up the phone, I felt lighter and my skin fit my body like it had never fit before. I could breathe. So many nights of struggling to take a good breath had taken its toll on me. The constant aching in my chest was a sign my anxiety was always lurking and I was reminded of it each time I would try and take a deep, relaxing breath. Even when my heart wasn't racing or my brain wasn't twitching with fear, my breathing would be affected. I just wanted to breathe. A visit to my medicine chest would usually give me temporary relief from this nagging irritation, but I only reserved those white pills for the nights when it was intolerable. I did not need to add a new set of problems to my already complicated mental and emotional life by popping Xanax like cocktail peanuts at a bar.

The moment I expressed how I was feeling to her, we unleashed a never ending barrage of emotions that would last for months. The fact that I was married, with children, and in this very interesting situation presented many challenges. In those early days, I felt the giddiness of a teenager who had just been asked to prom by the person they had their eye on. I was so grateful that even in the midst of the chaos of those first months I was able to put into words to how I was feeling. It was to her and reading it always reminds me that fairy tales are possible.

Feb 5, 2011

I've never composed a love story, however my life right now is the stuff love stories are made of. I am not sure I've ever known what that would look like; the fairy tale version never really appealed to my sensibilities. I am a highly practical and utilitarian person, also a realist in many ways, but my realism has given way to a less structured way lately. My current life story seems to be one there is no precedent for or one that any rea-

sonable person would be able to comprehend. This story is quickly becoming what may be my greatest of all time. The words to describe it may take some time to form and do it justice. I am finding it is beyond words, beyond description, and so sacred and holy of a thing that my heart is so full of love and gratitude. Words just are not enough. When I have a difficult time finding words, I have to rely on my senses and be sure to pay close attention to each moment as it unfolds. I am beyond grateful and so very blessed to have this amazing love with you. It is the greatest gift I have ever been given. I will protect it, nurture it, and hold it the most gentle and precious way I know how, because I am yours and you are mine. Above all else, we chose this to be, together, without hesitation. This I know for sure.

I cannot explain why the circumstances played out as they did. I do know, however, the day I met my best friend something shifted in me. I had no idea her friendship would forever change my journey and even less of an idea about how difficult navigating the road ahead would prove to be.

CHAPTER 3

Chaotic Peace

In the midst of movement and chaos,
keep the stillness inside of you.

— *Deepak Chopra*

N o, I did not always know this about myself. I honestly had no idea I was a lesbian. I wondered how it was possible to be unaware of this part of me and why it came to light when the stakes were so high and the impact so devastating. Forty years of my life had passed and learning this about myself could not have come at a more inconvenient time. Many times I sat in the silence and replayed everything in my mind. I approached things logically and rationally but could not come up with anything feasible. Was I that lost I did not even know myself? That would mean I was worse off than I had imagined. I was reminded by an old college friend that two years in to my marriage I had mentioned that my only regret about being married was that I never got to experience what it was like to be with a woman. What straight woman thinks this after getting married? What straight woman thinks this at all? It was a passing comment I had forgotten about. This seemed like a very large red flag I had missed early on in my marriage.

The first red flag, that I did not miss, happened six years prior to my coming out when I was struggling with severe anxiety and decided to undergo hypnosis. I was freaked out that my ex in laws had arranged a cruise for the entire family. I know, sounds like a great time, right? Not for me. I was terrified of getting on that boat and setting off for a week on the seas. As I look back, I can see how crazy this was. I have always loved the water and boats in particular. The idea of getting on a vessel I had no control over, however, proved to be too much for me to deal with. My fears were consuming me and there was no way I was going to ruin a vacation with my family because of my crippling anxiety.

In order to entertain the idea of going on that trip without the need for a straightjacket, heavy duty drugs, or both, I decided to try hypnosis. Yes, I needed to get on that boat, but also hoped it would help reduce my growing general level of anxiety. I was a hypnosis virgin and naturally nervous about the process. Honestly, there weren't too many things that didn't make me nervous during that time in my life. When I arrived at the hypnosis center, I was shown a lovely video explaining the science surrounding hypnosis. I suspect it was step one of the "cover your ass" liability waiver I would later sign. When the very informative video ended, I was led to a room off the conference area and instructed to take a seat in a big, brown chair. This chair reminded me of the one my grandfather had in his home many years ago. It was leather and had a foot rest that popped up when it reclined. From what I gathered from the video, relaxation was a key component of the process. Going in, I had my doubts about whether or not I was going to be able to relax. I also had to fight the thought that if this did not work it would be a complete waste of time and, more importantly, money. I felt a glimmer of hope for a positive experience when I realized how comfortable this chair felt when I plopped down into it.

Bob was my hypnotherapist. After I got settled in, he asked me what seemed like hundreds of questions. Seriously, this took at least thirty minutes out of my time slot. I hoped he knew what he was doing and I tried to be patient as he ran down the list of background questions. It was a very thorough intake process, for sure. He asked about my family and why I was there. Then he asked me the seemingly innocuous question, "Are you heterosexual or homosexual?"

My brain seized and images streaked across my mind that mirrored movie or television portrayals of hypnosis. I was certain there was a possibility of becoming the character in a bad Lifetime movie drama who suddenly uncovered some shocking memory or repressed truth. I immediately became afraid of what I had gotten myself into. These ridiculous ideas led my brain down a completely irrational path. It was a lovely mind trip I took in those initial moments.

When I snapped out of it, I answered with great indignation, "I am heterosexual." Had he not heard I was married and had three kids when he asked about my family four seconds earlier? I do not remember what the next series of questions were, let alone how I answered them, because my brain was still processing the question about my sexual orientation. After all of the questions were asked and answered, the needle on my record was skipping and I could not help but think, "Am I heterosexual?" I had never really asked myself or been asked that question before. Why was I thrown by that stupid question? From that point on, I was fearful that while I was in a relaxed and open state my subconscious mind would arrive at the conclusion I was gay before my conscious mind could handle the information. I was terrified but determined to let the process work. At that time, I was not interested in stirring up any new messes. I just needed to get on that boat.

I was surprised the session had the impact it did since I was so preoccupied and thrown by that one stupid question prior to starting. For those who have never experienced hypnosis, I highly recommend it. I was never more relaxed than while under hypnosis and it did result in positive progress with my anxiety levels. It also helped me to release the anger and negativity lingering from my childhood. For the skeptics out there, you will be happy to know I remember everything that happened and I did not leave there with an urge to cluck like a chicken every time I heard a car horn beep or a cell phone ring. It was not the kind of hypnosis corporations use to entertain their employees at annual meetings. I felt refreshed and for a short time was able to forget about the issue of why I was tripped up by the question about my sexual orientation.

I got on that boat and was less anxious in general, however there were moments when I still felt burdened by something I could not put my finger on. I underwent hypnosis a couple of more times because it was a great relaxation tool. I once again began seeing a therapist with the hopes of staying on track with the progress I had made. I was willing to look far and wide in order to find out and pin point what my problem was. Unbeknownst to me, my coming out process began on the couch at the hypnosis center. While I was not conscious of this at the time, I did notice changes taking place in me. Hindsight is a wonderful thing.

As my coming out process unfolded, my physical appearance underwent a transformation even though I was not consciously aware this was happening. There were external changes that accompanied my slowly changing internal thinking. As my relationship with myself improved, the changes in my thinking manifested themselves outwardly. I finally had a sense of self and the ironic thing was as a result I looked and felt more feminine than I had in my entire life.

From the moment I got tripped up in my first hypnosis session, I put the possibility I could be gay on the back burner. Actually, I shut off the gas to the stove, put the lid on the pot, and tried to forget about it. I could not entertain the thought. As it became more apparent this was the case, I tried everything to make this NOT be the case. If I could just love my husband more and do more for him, this would go away. It had to be some kind of sign my marriage was suffering, but it was not.

I took a couple of months to wrap my brain around the fact that I was a lesbian. I spent many moments contemplating what it all meant. The time between when I realized I was gay and when I told my husband came in stages. The events transpired over a six month period, but it would take years to adjust to this revelation. Each phase of time had a certain feel. The first few months were a time when I allowed myself to just be and slowly make sense of everything. It was an amazing yet terrifying few months. I needed time to wrap my brain around the magnitude of the situation. I carefully considered all of the things that were going to change for not only myself, but for my family. It felt like it was my time to try to get a small grip on what was unfolding in my life. Finding out the world as you have known it for your entire life was about to be completely changed was shocking, exciting and incredibly sad at the same time.

Once I came to a place of understanding and made the decision to out myself, I was terrified but certain. I did not look forward to what I knew this would mean for my family. I had a resolve I had never felt before even knowing the mess this would create. I enjoyed these few months because I was completely confident I had figured out my truth. At the same time, I also dreaded what I knew needed to be done in my marriage. I was never interested in keeping it a secret or hiding my sexuality from the world. Go big or go home, right? My search for authenticity reached its peak and for me to be true to myself required living in the light of day and sharing my news with everyone. I did not stand in the city center and shout from a rooftop. I was cautious as I slowly revealed my truth to the people in my world. The first person I told was a man I trusted and had known for many years.

Toes in the Sand

The day I spoke the words "I am gay" out loud to someone, aside from my best friend, is hazy. I was present but it felt l like I was observing from afar. I could not believe the words were about to come out of my mouth — pun intended. I was sure I had to do this and wondered if I would be able to let those words pass my lips.

I called my friend the night before and told him I needed to talk. He could tell something was not right. He asked me if I was ok. I told him I could not go into detail because I had my family milling about. He again asked if I was ok. I told him I was but I did not think anyone else was going to be. The next morning we met at a busy diner in town. I remember my heart racing and feeling like my head was floating when I saw him walk in the door. We sat in a booth and for a few minutes I didn't say anything. He just looked at me and waited. I think I said something about not knowing where to start or how to do this. Then I just said it out loud. Once the words "I'm gay" come from your mouth there is no back pedaling. I barely got the words out and then came tears. His reply to me was "Been a long time coming, huh?" which I thought was a bit strange. I just nodded and felt the lump in my throat grow. I realized what he had said was true. The tears falling from my eyes were tears of relief and fear.

I cannot recall any details or specifics about what was said the rest of the time we spoke. In the midst of this emotional conversation, I vividly recall hearing the song "Toes in the Sand" playing while we sat in the diner. The song reminded me of my husband, the trips we took to Key West, and our vacations at the beach. The image of him relaxing and living the words of the song were such a stark contrast to what his life would become once I told him my news. I hated that I would be the one responsible for shattering his peace. I just sat there with the tears rolling down my cheeks as I considered this very painful image. Even years later, hearing that song provokes the memory of that day.

The biggest blessing that morning was I did not walk away feeling condemned. This man was a deacon at my church and was a close friend to our family. My husband and I had a very good relationship with him and his wife. We had served on the pre-cana team with them for many years. I knew he was the one I needed to tell and that he would listen. He was cool that way. If I think about it hard enough, I do recall him encouraging me to take one thing at a time and offering me reassurance that everything was going to be okay. I knew deep down eventually things would be okay, but I had no idea exactly when that would be.

It was ironic that, as he and I spoke, I looked up and saw one of the priests from the parish had come in for breakfast. This particular clergyman was keenly aware of the two of us being there and sat on the other side of the diner. He was a busy body type and sure enough later that day, from what I am told, made one of his usual sarcastic statements to the deacon asking if he enjoyed the counseling session that morning with me. He was rude that way. Later down the road, when the news broke at church, this same priest sat and told me I needed to be careful because this was going to be a problem for me in the future. In that moment, I knew exactly where I stood with the Church.

I left the diner and heeded the advice I had just received to let things sit for a day or so. It was a long couple of days. The next steps were telling my husband, my kids, and then the world. The months that led up to my telling the deacon were filled with tears, unbelievable joy, and a sense of finally embracing the unknown. I finally knew I had reached the point in my journey where I felt free. It is a strange experience going from feeling bound for so long without really being able to put your finger on why to feeling such a sense of freedom.

The next person on the list of people to share this with was my husband. I knew this would be difficult for me to do. I chose to tell him one night after my youngest son's baseball game. As I stood on the field photographing, I distinctly remember looking over at him where he sat. I could not help thinking about how his life would be turned upside down. I was terrified. I wondered what I would say, how he would react, and what life would look like in just a few short hours for us both. The adrenaline was coursing through my body and I just wished I could find someone else to do this for me.

Even though I had these thoughts running through my mind, I knew it had to be done. Knowing this truth was not going to disappear and that I was not having a midlife crisis or living in a horrible marriage only made it more difficult. I was gay and nothing was going to change that. Realizing no one would literally die from this was of little comfort. I had to keep telling myself this or else I did not know how I was going to get through it all. I knew this curve ball would take the batter by surprise and would strike a blow to the very place where things that were supposed to be forever were kept. This pitch would come in like a wrecking ball demolishing the side of a brick building. How would I be able to live with myself? I knew ending the personal battle going on in my head was important enough reason to cause all of this emotional fallout. My heart and mind had been suffocated by unrest long enough and it was not anybody's fault. I knew I had to take the leap of faith and I was willing to take whatever fallout would shower from the skies above in order to stand in my truth.

I will never forget the moment when I told my husband that I was gay. The way life felt after I told him changed. It was like remembering where you were on 9-11. Events in life can serve as markers in time. We all enjoy the happy ones, like an amazing vacation or the birth of a child, but sometimes there are sad ones, like a death or tragedy. My coming out to him was strangely both. Replaying the scene in my mind, it is difficult to remember the exact words exchanged between the two of us. I can still see flashes of images, like snapshots in a scrapbook, and remember the smell of the pool water. I recall the candle light flickering on his face and his expression afterwards haunted me for a very long time. I remember him asking me questions, but I had no answers. So many moments during the conversation I wished I was someone else, or that this was not happening, or that I could be anywhere else on the planet. We cried as he wanted to know what this meant for our future.

I only managed to tell him things would be different. In this conversation, I did not mention I was in love with someone else. I thought this would be too much for him to take in at that moment. I regret my decision to omit this from our conversation, but I honestly wanted to protect him as much as

I could while he absorbed the reality his wife was gay. Neither of us slept that night. He could not eat, focus on work, or even wrap his brain around what had just happened. I knew once I told him about her things would only become more complicated. I felt like a criminal, yet I knew I had to do this if I was going to have peace in my life. I have never once regretted the decision to share my truth and act on this self-awareness. Even in the ugliest moments of this whole event, I have never questioned my decision. I could not see myself remaining married and denying this part of myself. It wouldn't have been fair to any of us.

I did struggle with the suffering this man had to experience in order for me to free my mind from the chains it was bound by. The days immediately following seemed to last forever. I spent many of those early days dealing with a man who, up until the day I came out to him, had never seemed to suffer an ounce of anxiety in his life. Now he was emotionally wrecked and it was all my doing. I believe I actually witnessed what a heart looks like when it is shattered into a million pieces. The aftermath was so hard to watch.

Life became a roller coaster of emotions. Having to go about the regular daily grind knowing everything was changing sucked. There were baseball games to attend, work projects to complete, and hundreds of mundane tasks that seemed so ridiculous given the circumstance. My revelation was a perspective changer. There were late nights figuring out how this could be happening. We shook our heads and wondered how our future together could be gone. We tried to understand how the plans we had made would never be realized and how this was not what either of us had planned for ourselves. What could I do?

I offered whatever sleeping pills and anxiety meds I had on hand, which did little to calm his distraught heart. I did my best to listen and be compassionate and caring. I kept thinking if the shoe was on the other foot I probably would not like the situation either. I did not want to be the cause of any more discomfort to this kind man who had been my husband for 17 years, so I took over everything. He never asked for any of this, but then again, neither did I. I did what I always did. I made him as comfortable as I could despite the circumstances. I entertained the idea I was bisexual and not gay upon his suggestion and listened to him plan how we could just work this out. How we could stay together for the kids.

The bottom line was whatever the plans had been, they were not any longer. I had to follow this new path. There was a part of me that knew how difficult it was going to be for our family to move forward. I also knew it was going to be even more difficult for me to figure out how to live as a lesbian in the world we live in today. My whole life was on its way to an overhaul that only a fool would choose willingly. I seriously could not believe this was happening to my married life. I wondered what signs I missed. I wondered where those people who shared they were not surprised when they heard my news had been months, even years, ago.

Did I really not know myself to such an extent that it had come to this? At times, my anger was directed at God and at others it was directed inward. I wished He would have seen fit to reveal this truth to me before I had married, if nothing else than to spare my husband and children this unexpected and devastating news. I have never been one to enjoy imparting pain, misery, or sadness on those I love. This was not something any of them deserved and I found myself feeling like the grim reaper of my family. I yelled at God, at my husband, and at myself very often in those early days.

In the mess however, was a sense of contentment I had prayed and longed for over many years. My own anxiety lessened to a point I actually felt the empty space it left when it lifted. This place was mine and its address was on the opposite side of the world from the emotional house my husband was in. The most amazing thing to me is even in the midst of the giant mess, I felt peace.

CHAPTER 4

Broken Hearts

It is time for parents to teach young people early on that in diversity there is beauty and there is strength.

— *Maya Angelou*

T he idea of coming out to my young children haunted me for months. I knew it would be a shock to them and there would be a lot of processing to do as they dealt with my homosexuality. Before the kids knew about my being a lesbian, I would become physically ill at the thought of telling them. I absolutely hated knowing I was going to be the root cause of their lives changing. I never saw myself being divorced and never wanted my kids to have to deal with their family going through something so difficult. There is a grieving process children naturally experience regardless of the reason why their parent's divorce. My kids were not immune from this, but they would have to deal with a double whammy. The entire situation was made worse because my marriage was not tumultuous or filled with high drama.

Telling my kids their father and I were no longer going to be married and their mother was a lesbian is tied for first on my list of hardest things I've ever had to do. The actual conversation with the kids took place three months after I told my husband. We knew telling the kids would only add layers to the emotional mess we were already dealing with as a couple. I had wanted to talk to the kids as soon as possible as we sorted through what this meant for our marriage. If it had been up to me, I would have dropped this bomb on the day my youngest made his First Communion. Most of our closest family and friends were going to be at the house and I thought it would be a good opportunity to rip off the bandage. I was vetoed and eventually conceded it would probably have been an epic disaster. It was so difficult to pretend everything was normal when so much was going on.

We waited until the children were out of school so they could react as they needed to free from the pressure of homework and out of the view of their peers. I dreaded the possible rejection I faced once they knew. My sons were 14, 12, and 8 at the time. It was May 31st and as parents we both knew it was time. I knew this was going to create spider web cracks in the windshield of their lives which would obstruct their view going forward. I worried about how this would affect them now and in the long run. I worried what their friends would say and, more importantly, how my being a lesbian would impact their worldview. I about worried if any bitterness or anger would affect them in the future.

My husband and I spent many hours locked in the den discussing, crying, and figuring out what this was going to look like as we moved forward. We both were nervous about informing the boys. There was a heaviness in our house and they could sense something was happening. I could only imagine how difficult it was for them to feel like something was not right but not have a clue as to what it was. Kids have a keen intuition and when something is amiss, their gauges register it like a barometer registers an approaching hurricane.

Shaking their foundation was never on my list of things to do as a mother. They needed to know the truth despite how hard and sickening it was to think about. We consulted professionals regarding the best way to go about having this difficult conversation. We hashed out what to tell them, the right words to use, and the words to avoid. We discussed who would say what and which one of us would comfort them if they became upset. It felt like we were preparing for a corporate presentation. They knew something was up immediately when we wanted to talk to them on the patio. That was a place reserved for pool parties, cook outs, and just relaxing. I remember looking at the two older ones as they sat on the patio couch waiting to hear what we were about to tell them. That single moment in time is frozen in my memory. I wanted to remember what they looked like in that instant because I wasn't sure they would ever be the same after they heard what we were about to tell them.

We told our older kids first so we sent our youngest to be with his grandmother. The children's ages dictated different conversations so we chose to do it in two parts. The next few hours were unforgettable. We each took a deep breath and laid it out for them in the most gentle way we could. We told them we loved them and we had some things to talk about. "Are we in trouble?" one asked. "Is it good or bad?" the other asked. "No, you are not in trouble and it is not good or bad." I replied. Their dad told them "Your mom and I are getting a divorce." Blank stares followed. In the silence, I added "The reason why this is happening is that I am gay." The oldest thought we were joking. We liked to joke about things with our kids, and I think this was his way of hoping what he was being told wasn't the truth. Then he just sat, silent, staring off at the pool water. He would not speak. He had no questions and just shut down. At one point, I noticed a tear trickle down his cheek. He soon disappeared into his room. I did not know if he would ever come out.

My middle son just wailed in grief after learning we were not going to be together and were getting a divorce. He told us he couldn't believe this was happening to him. My heart broke and ached for him. He continued to cry for a long time, alternating between laying on our bed and the living room floor. He was hysterical and could not cope. It was one of the most disturbing things I have ever seen.

When it was time for the youngest to return home, we asked the other two to not let him know the news yet. I hated that we had just dropped this information on them a few hours earlier and now were asking them to pull it together when their brother came home. I did not like interrupting their processing time, but as parents we needed time to recover and prepare for telling the only person in the house who did not know what was happening. They agreed. When their little brother walked in the door, they greeted him and acted like it was a normal evening in our house. The most beautiful thing happened next. On a normal day, these brothers would typically be bugging one another just for the sport of it. On this difficult day, I saw the depth of their bond with one another as they interacted with the little guy. I could tell they wanted to protect him from the devastating information they had just learned. They pulled themselves together for the sake of their baby brother. It was amazing. I saw the strength and grace they each had under this uninvited circumstance and I knew they would both be okay one day. I had a sense this would not be the thing that rearranged their emotional DNA and had hope this family storm would not rob them of their peace forever.

The days following were a series of emotional breakdowns because they did not know what to do with the deep emotions of it all. One moment, they were brave little men. Next, they were fiercely bickering with one another. It was like a mine field of emotions for every one of us, every day. It was now safe for the truth to become public knowledge. We had kept the veil of secrecy over this for the children's sake. We had not wanted anyone to know about the change in our family situation before the kids did. It was important that we were the primary source of this information. It had to come from us. Can you imagine what it would have been like if they had found out from someone else?

Once my kids were told, we began slowly and carefully sharing our news with the rest of the world. We offered reassurance to everyone who implored us to make sure the kids were taken care of emotionally. We were highly offended by these conversations. We always operated with the best interest of our kids in mind and resented the insinuation we would not take care of them in all of this. Our track record on this was clear. We cocooned ourselves as we sought to protect our whole family's delicate emotional state. We made sure people understood we considered everything we were advised to do. We were irritated when people thought we would take a "fly by the seat of the pants" approach with our children. We had no patience for friendly advice when it came to addressing concerns about our kid's welfare. We had it handled.

A couple of weeks after the kids were told, we began the task of officially undoing our marriage. The next step in our journey was changing the face of what each of our lives looked like together and separately.

Saint Augustine

Many months prior to any of this happening, my husband and I had planned a vacation for our anniversary. It would be a celebration of our 17 years as a married couple. He decided we should keep our plan but change the destination. I secretly dreaded this trip. I knew the emotions we were about to go through would feel so raw and strong. I wondered if either of us could emerge from them without permanent scars.

I have never considered St. Augustine, Florida among my favorite places. Ever. I had visited on a few occasions prior to our "marriage wrap up"- "business meeting" and was never a fan. Granted, there are beautiful buildings everywhere and the entire area has such historical significance. It is home to the oldest wooden school house in the United States, the Fountain of Youth, and Flagler College. There is a very well-known old fort, Castillo De San Marcos that is a main attraction for fourth grade field trips. Yet, while I can appreciate the history of the area, I have never been wowed by it all. Honestly, for me it is an old and not very interesting locale to visit.

It was the first place I thought of to go to for our last trip as a couple. I did not want to go somewhere I enjoyed because I knew wherever I went would quickly find itself atop the list of places to avoid in the future. The ghost of my marriage would be joining the ranks of other ghosts in that old city. It was the perfect place to leave the energy that consumed us that weekend. Looking back, it was an ironic choice. I consider this my contribution to the history of St. Augustine.

Our first night, we shopped and reminisced. It was oddly normal and felt like the hundreds of shopping trips we had made together in the past. It was comfortably uncomfortable. The whole time I knew this would most likely be the last time we took a trip with each other alone. Once we arrived at the hotel, the entire look and feel of the weekend was more like a funeral than a vacation. It was like being at your own wake, fully alert to every feeling, thought, and emotion imaginable. The range of emotions was overwhelming. The sadness at the loss of our marriage was so palpable, especially in the quiet moments.

The most difficult thing for me was I really loved this man. He had been my partner and we had grown up together in our marriage. We had championed each other all the way through. We had always kept kindness in our hearts whenever we hit bumps in the road. I can honestly say he never called me a name in all of our time together, from when we were dating to the day I told him about my being gay. Not once did he demean me. He was my cheerleader and my friend. I could not have chosen a better father for my children. All this made everything so damn hard to swallow.

Even these things, though true, were not enough to squash my need to go forward. It was dusk and the only color my eyes registered was the gray hue in the horizon signaling the change from light to dark. We had conversations walking on the beach about what the kids' arrangements would look like, when I would move out, how to split up the things we had built together financially and materially. I literally felt my heart break more than once that weekend. I dropped to my knees when he thanked me for my efforts to try to make this not be the case and for loving him the way I did. He offered me his shirt as we walked because I was chilly. I could not believe in the midst of that walk, given what we were discussing, he would do such a kind thing for the woman who was turning his world upside down. We sat in a lifeguard stand and simply cried. There were no words in that moment that could have conveyed for either of us the magnitude of the situation and our emotions. I was drained and emotionally exhausted after the weekend. The only thing that remained in me was the sting of what would never be and the thoughts about how this was not supposed to be the plan for our lives.

He knew I had not asked for this and I had not always known this. I was restless within myself and realized I had settled into a life that didn't feel like it had much meaning. I played wife and mother, but some days I had a hard time finding Dawn in it all. I became my roles and my responsibilities. My life seemed to be decided for me. My days were filled with activities, commitments, and expectations of what I was to everyone. I felt empty and alone, and could not shake it. I discovered what I wanted and what I had did not match. My coming out was the first step in reclaiming my life as it was supposed to have been. My spirit had felt disjointed and disconnected from itself for a very long time. I finally was able to face the reality I was absent in my own life. I wondered why finding me meant such a drastic change, but I was never more certain of anything in my life.

During our weekend, I would see older couples out and about and would tear up because it would never be us. The incredible guilt and responsibility I felt for devastating this man who had been nothing but kind to me for so many years was overwhelming. Yet I knew deep down this was all part of the grieving process. Our marriage had been dying a slow death. Even though the weekend was filled with gut wrenching emotions and rivers of tears, I knew it was all part of the process. I just wanted to move forward for me. Because the weight was so heavy, I was afraid at times if I stopped moving forward I would cease to be. I missed her. I could only imagine what she was feeling when I was gone that weekend. I wanted to be able to get to a place where I could sit comfortably in my own earth suit.

When your life looks one way on Monday and then looks completely different on Tuesday, it is hard. Flipping the tables is messy. It was very hard for me to imagine the day when things would be "normal," when the crying would stop and the anger and fear would disappear. I wondered when, if ever, the grief and mourning would be over. I knew this was my truth, but I still felt bound by the mess I created when I came out. It was like living two separate lives. I had my new life with the knowledge I was a lesbian. I felt energy coursing through me like I had never experienced before — a nervous and highly charged energy which was exciting and exhilarating.

On the other hand, I felt drained and exhausted. I knew what this admission had brought but was unsure of how to clean up the collateral damage. Taking the new route was not easy, I could not just change lanes and get off on a new and exciting exit forgetting the road I had just been on. It was a mess. Plain and simple. This mess reached a level of cluster fuck I had never seen before or imagined possible. Yet it was mine and I had a part in creating it.

CHAPTER 5

Emotional Rollercoaster

*Don't grieve. Anything you lose comes round
in another form.*

— *Rumi*

O nce I shared with my husband I had developed a relationship with my best friend, everything was out in the open. We were all experiencing the same thing and knew we needed to work together as things unfolded especially for the kids' sake. The adults who initially committed to be a team were my ex-husband, her, and me. Her ex was having a never ending tantrum which went on for months. Based on the unpredictable behavior of her spouse, the three of us decided we would dictate how this went by loving each other like we had on the day before this all came to pass. We had the sense to realize if we were going to get through this we would need to rally around each other to survive whatever the world would throw our way. We were completely aware the husbands would be the "poor schmucks" and we would be the proud, permanent owners of shiny, new villain suits. She and I would don our home wrecker belts with matching handbags ready to defend our deviant and morally reprehensible lifestyle to the world. I wish I were kidding about this. There were conclusions made about us and we all had to contend with the accompanying fallout.

Things happened very quickly from the time the kids were told to the time I actually moved out of the house. I secured a home to rent about a mile away from the family house. I did this with the hopes of minimizing the disruption to the kids. Their school bus would not change so they would just have to get off at the next stop to come to my house afterschool. I had days where I felt like I had one foot in his house and the other in my own house after I moved out. If I could have split myself into two people, I would have. It would have been easier that way to do what I needed to do. The responsibility of everything fell upon my hands. I agreed to take on the whole enchilada — finances, household logistics, paperwork, and everything related to the kids — but in time I resented it.

I had forgotten it was not my job to atone for this unexpected turn in life. I remembered after one long night spent crying I had a right to be happy and to go forward. My feelings of obligation were not healthy for me to continue acting on. My moving out of the house took a toll on each of us. There would be moments of being okay and then, without warning, the entire face of the moment would change. Added to the mix was the fact that everyone seemed to have an opinion. Whether they shared it with us or not was irrelevant. He was counseled about being too nice to me. I was counseled to make sure I protected myself financially since I had chosen to stay at home and raise the children. We were told to get a good lawyer and not to tell the kids the whole truth. We received so much unsolicited advice in those early weeks both of us could not even begin to sort it all. We knew what we had to do in order to get through this. The split and separation were as amicable as they come. We loved each other and, from the beginning, we honestly wished happiness for the other even under the weight of the circumstance. It was not an act. Even though this path was not what we had expected for our lives, we knew in time we would both be healed because of the way we loved one another. We did not care what the world thought. We would work this out in our own way. The truth would set us all free even if it took some time to get there.

Six months from the day I told my husband I was gay, we were officially divorced. As we moved forward, we were still together. We slowly began the difficult separation process in our heads. We had the same attorney and worked out all of the details as we formulated our dissolution of marriage. Our first meeting with the lawyer was quick. The process was uneventful and like a business meeting. We were civil and kind as we finalized the paperwork, but we were both heartbroken. I wondered if the lawyer who was drafting the end of our marriage was completely confused by our decision given how kind we were to one another. When the time came to sign the papers, I thought it would be easier than it ended up being. I remember that day so vividly.

The weather was horrible. As I made the ten mile drive north to the lawyer's office, the sky was dark and rain began to pelt my van. I was clearly headed into a storm. It was as if how I felt on the inside was being played out in the clouds. The emotional hurricane ravaging my insides had somehow seeped out into the atmosphere. It was too much to bear. The waves of sadness rolled over me and I knew while I was sure of my path from this point on I had never felt so devastated. As I got closer to the office, I passed by so many places that held meaning for us as a couple. It was a ride filled with flashbacks of so many shared times. Most notable was passing by the street that led to the state park where we had been married 17 years earlier

I remember seeing him exit his car at the lawyer's office and thinking he had never looked more handsome than on that day. We were both sure this was how it had to be in order for us to find our own happiness separately. Our eyes were sad but we still smiled. I think on some level we both were in disbelief this was actually happening. The day we signed the final papers was one of the saddest days of my life. I could not help thinking that this was not supposed to go this way. We both felt like failures and emotionally fell apart. We had maintained a certainty during our whole marriage that we would always be together and it had not come to pass. I was angry. He was angry and hurt. He would look at married couples he thought weren't as great as us and felt cheated they got to have what he had wanted — forever. We would never be that cute old couple still holding hands while taking a stroll. There was so much that would never be and it was hard to wrap my brain and heart around that.

We sat in the freezing cold conference room and just cried. When the lawyer returned with the papers for us to sign, the tears did not stop. Again, he at times looked very confused as to why this was necessary for two people who clearly loved each other. We never explained the circumstances surrounding the divorce. It was not necessary and I did not want or need one more person looking at me like a villain. I felt bad enough. We finished and left without saying a word. We exchanged a tearful hug at our cars and headed to our separate homes.

On the way home, I was a wreck. I barely remember the ride other than the sound of my sniffling breaking the silence in the car every few minutes. I was glad he had the kids that week because the rest of the night I would spend inconsolable and inside my own internal heartache. It was strange that I could only remember the good times that day, which seemed cruel. I was feeling every emotion which was a good thing given that feeling emotions isn't my strong suit. I sat on my youngest son's bed that night and wept. The huge, hot tears ran down my face and I felt so empty. This process of grieving was very new to me. I did not want it to be how it was. We had our share of regular marital issues. We were very different in many ways and those differences were becoming more apparent with every passing year.

I cannot say with certainty if I had not been gay we would have ended up happily ever after. We had a conversation not long after I came out where we both came to the conclusion our getting married was probably something we should not have done. This realization was not a source of hurt for either of us but more of an acknowledgement that, while we were a good team, there were things "off" in our marriage independent of my discovering I was a lesbian. The tears were for the loss of what I thought would be and not a sadness about wanting to have my marriage back. I did not want what I had back. I needed to grieve this to move forward.

As I went through the hardest year of my life and dealt with the ramifications of this awareness, I felt everything. I struggled at times with being able to verbalize what emotion I was feeling, but was determined to stay aware and committed to getting around to it eventually. I experienced happy tears as well as angry and sad ones. I realized part of my journey through this time took me through a grieving process. I hoped I could get through it all with some measure of grace and dignity, taking each day as it came. I hoped at some point down the road all would be well. Did I mention I didn't have a good grip on what grief looks like in my own life?

I have never been the type who falls apart when somebody else does. I feel like being there for someone and understanding their pain in those very tender moments without falling apart is a helpful thing. In my infinite wisdom, I have learned that sometimes crying along with someone is just as helpful to them as it is to me. I have learned the hard way that blocking emotions and stuffing hurt or pain inside is not tough; it takes a great deal of strength and courage to be able to feel things as they come. God has a funny way of teaching us these very basic truths. Our emotions are a key ingredient in the recipe that is our humanity. Without question, coming out has been a lesson in this. I am not ashamed to admit that I have fallen apart more times in the last year than I had in my entire life.

I can honestly say I did grieve my marriage. That process began long before I ever told another person that I was gay. I knew because this was my truth I could not remain married to my husband. I had to quietly come to terms with this before I was able to move forward in my life. I could have stayed the prescribed course and denied my authentic self out of the obligation and promise I made when I married, but that would not have been good for either of us.

As everything unfolded, I was surprised by some of the things that I felt a loss about. My house was one of them. I found it very difficult to understand how I could grieve an inanimate object. I moved out of the home that my husband and I built for our growing family. I missed my house. It was dumb, but true. The house was my first home and I played a big part in how it looked. I lived there for almost eleven years. I never put much stock in material things and was always of the mind that home is in your heart and not where you hang your hat. My heart, however, missed where I used to hang my hat. I did not realize I would miss things about the house which had nothing to do with décor. I missed the neighborhood and the dear friends living there.

In my analytical and rational mind, I figured wherever I went would become my new home. I was wrong. The rental home was where we hung our hats, but it was a reminder of the chaos that coming out brought. Two years after I came out, I bought a home down the street from it. This is where my heart is. Each time I leave my home, I have to pass right in front of that rental house and am reminded of our time there. The rental house was the place where my wife and I began our life together. It was a safe place for us to work through everything that had happened as well as a place where we were able to laugh and create a new normal.

My process of mourning was not a function of wanting what I had back. I think for many people this view of grieving is a foreign one. My grief took the form of adjusting to change. I had gained so much through this process. I am past asking questions like "why did this happen so late in life for me?" or "how could I have not realized this before I married and began my family?" Knowing the why does not help change it or make sense of things. I have found that line of thinking to be more confusing in the end. Why is irrelevant at times. What I do in the present is truly the important piece of the puzzle.

Going through the grieving process during the first year after coming out gave me so many glimpses into what grief is and the many forms it could take. In my situation, no one had died. I realized any change in life's circumstances can bring about a sense of grief. I have learned loss is loss and is not always relegated to when someone physically dies. I have watched many people grieve in my life; friends who lost children, parents, spouses, family members, and friends. These people have had their lives turned upside down without any notice or warning. Others knew a loss was near. I always thought grieving was a response to someone dying. No one had died, yet there was so much mourning going on for each of us who went through this experience.

As hard as it was to navigate the debris field in my own home, it was even harder to watch the hell my best friend went through during that period of time. Typically when major things happened we relied on each other to get through them. We were both experiencing our own personal hell. I was struggling to keep things together as the walls fell down around me. Knowing her circumstance in her own house had escalated to a very disturbing level after the gay bomb was dropped, was heartbreaking. The worst part was there was nothing I could do to help alleviate the complete chaos her coming out had unleashed. To say things did not go well would be an understatement. The only visual that best captures what the three months after her coming out were like would be if the beginning scenes of the movie *Saving Private Ryan* were combined with the final baptism scene from the first *Godfather* movie. Instead of classical music, the soundtrack would have been sung by Marilyn Manson.

He promised to destroy her and take everything from her. He vowed to sell every stick of furniture to make sure she had nothing. He threatened to take her car, then demanded she tell him who paid for her lawyer or he would not sign over the car. He emptied their joint account and left her with nothing before the divorce papers had even been filed. This was a far cry from the initial calm reaction he had shown when she first told him. Only after a few weeks did the anger, hate, and threats begin. She did not leave because she knew he would never let her take her son with her and she did not want to put her child in the middle of an already dangerous and quickly escalating situation. Her ex became unhinged. He watched every move she made and took every opportunity to make sure her son knew what a terrible mother she was. He would keep her up at night and not let her sleep. Everywhere she went, he went. He eavesdropped on her phone conversations and questioned everything she did.

On one occasion I had to go to her home. He was there waiting for me and interrogated me for a couple of hours. He threatened to physically throw me out of his house and I told him to do it. Again, my mouth was running. He decided to pick up the phone and call my husband to tell him to come get me off of his property. I refused. The thing about her ex was that he was big on making threats but terrible on the follow through. I did not leave and he proceeded to insult my husband because he was being a "pussy" and not acting like a real man. I was not going to leave her alone with him until he calmed down. Eventually things settled to the point where things had cooled off and, after four hours, I went home. I wanted her to come with me because I knew in the pit of my stomach he was going to amp it up the moment I left. I was right.

She was distraught and had no way out. When she finally moved out, she had her mom sit in the living room so there would be a buffer between the two of them. As she went through things that were hers, he would look through everything to see what she was taking. She left the house with her clothes and the few personal possessions he allowed her to remove from the home. By the time she was out of the house, she looked like a soldier who had just come home from war. She was emotionally, physically, and mentally exhausted. She weighed 96 pounds and looked like hell.

In the end, he got the house, the bank accounts, and her kid. Mission accomplished. He signed the car over after a long and drawn out battle that included her having to put a club on the car while she was at work. (He had suggested he was going to sell her car so that he could pay for his lawyer.) It took almost a year for their divorce papers to be signed and then another few months for the settlement to be finalized. She was blamed for the delays. In the end, she was awarded half of his pension and did get to keep her car. Everything was always her fault. This had been the general theme of their marriage. It killed me to have to watch her go through this nightmare. It is so hard to watch someone I love deal with her son wanting nothing to do with her.

The way things played out in her situation illustrated the ugly side of what happens when a spouse comes out and a marriage ends. Her marriage did not end any differently than it had been for many years. This just amplified it. Controlling people have a very difficult time handling situations they cannot control which is often the case in emotionally abusive relationships. One of the happiest days for me was the day she was able to move into the rental home. I soon joined her and she was finally able to begin the process of healing. My wife did the hardest thing a mom could do when she agreed to let her son live with his dad. This decision was made out of love and consideration for her son's wellbeing. It broke her heart. There were so many attempts to make things bearable for him, but he was just not in a place to embrace our new life. This experience afforded all of us a plethora of opportunities to practice the difficult task of letting go.

When my son was sick I learned to let go of the things I could not control and to trust God. I learned I was stronger than I ever imagined. Whatever the outcome would have been, it would have been okay. I am beyond thankful I did not lose this child. I took away from this experience the mindset that every life is a gift and that life is full of challenges. I spent many years grieving what he had to go through, even though he was still here with us. I have had my big girl tantrums in the past about "why him," since this is something he will have to deal with for his lifetime. He is on medication and when he was eight had the missing valve replaced. There is the possibility he will most likely need to have the original valve replaced due to the fact that it was not perfect either and scar tissue has formed over time. Over time, my tantrums subsided and I chose to look at each day as a blessing. I always remember for as sick as he was, there were other children much sicker who did not go home with their parents. I learned no matter what may be happening, it could always be worse. Coming out could have been yet another opportunity to wear my victim suit.

His health scare helped me to focus on the big picture in whatever I may be facing. When having a bad day, I only had to remember what living in a hospital room felt like for six weeks. Showering in a hall bathroom and not knowing when my son would be leaving seemed like the worse it could get. Having something break on the car seems like a gift in comparison. I have had a visual reminder of this pop up many times over the years. We live in a small community about two hours from where he was in the hospital. The little boy who happened to be in the room next to my son was one year old. While I was in the hospital with my son, I noticed this boy's parents were not there much. I found it odd they were not at his bedside, but understood life went on and the boy was receiving the best care possible from the nurses and doctors at the hospital. I'd see the parents on weekends and pass them in the cafeteria. We were cordial and friendly to one another. When my son was discharged, we came home to our newly built house and life rolled along. I had no idea the other couple lived in our town. I saw her a couple of months later at our local grocery store and hesitantly asked how her son was doing. He had died. My heart broke for her and I felt so blessed our son was still with us. From that day, I prayed for her because she looked so deeply affected by it. You could see the devastation in her eyes and the loss in her face.

God has a funny way of reminding us to count our blessings when we least expect it. Over a dozen years have passed and I have seen the boy's mother in the store more times than I can count. I don't look like I did back then and I am sure she has no idea who I am, but I will never forget her. Each time I have seen her, there's a moment where my brain returns to those very rough days. I am immediately back in the hospital. I can smell the room and hear the sounds. It would hit me every single time that my son is doing okay and is here with us while hers is not. The moment has served as a reminder to me that no matter what kind of mood or day I am having I am blessed and have been spared the grief she has known. About a year ago I saw her again, in another store, and she was pushing a stroller with a gorgeous baby boy in it. She was with her mom and I shed a tear of joy as I passed by the aisle they were in. This was a beautiful day.

I believe to some degree I am still grieving the loss of my straightness, as ridiculous as this may sound. Man and wife is a traditional, socially acceptable relationship. I mourn the loss of the freedom attached to being in a "normal" relationship. There is a safety in marriage with regard to how the world views me that I no longer have the luxury of. Whatever gains in acceptance being gay has made in society in recent years, a great majority still believe that by nature it is wrong, deviant and unholy. The fact that I have "chosen" to be in a relationship with another woman has become the primary filter by which I am viewed every day. Fortunately, there are those in my life for whom this is not an issue, but there were relationships that changed due to my coming out. When I began spreading the word about my new way of living, I quickly added relationships to my list of things to be mourned.

CHAPTER 6

Awkward Silence

*He who does not understand your silence will probably
not understand your words.*

— *Elbert Hubbard*

I stared at my phone. I needed to decide how I was going to tell the rest
of my family and friends what was happening. I sat for what seemed like
hours trying to figure out where I should start. As a consummate planner, I
wondered if I should I blurt out the news or ease into it? Should I open with
a joke? I tried to carefully craft a concise and appropriate script I could work
from when it came time to share my news. I just wanted to get the facts out
and be done with. I didn't think I could handle comforting anyone who
might become upset by what they were about to hear. I was not emotionally ready to field a barrage of questions or partake in any lengthy conversations on those first calls.

The first conversations I had were with my immediate family. I covered
all of the bases. I began with the news I was divorcing. This information was
shocking in and of itself because to others there were not any warning signs
my marriage was tanking. As they began to react to that news, I would cut
them off and let them know I had more to tell them. Then I hit them with

the fact that I was gay. I had a hard time labeling myself as a lesbian in the beginning. I was still getting used to the term myself, so I used the word gay to convey the gist of it. I delivered the information in a very clinical and matter of fact way.

The reactions to my sudden announcement were interesting, sometimes surprising, but mostly expected. My dad's reaction mirrored my delivery and his responses were very encouraging to me. He has always been one of my biggest fans. My dad and I are the most alike in my family and have always had a close relationship. To this day he still calls me by my childhood nickname, Monkey, which I love. His support was not surprising at all. When I told him I was getting a divorce and that I was gay, he said, "This does not change anything, Monk. You are my daughter. When you were married to a guy I did not think of you as my straight daughter. You were my daughter. I do not think of you as my gay daughter now. You are my daughter. As long as you are happy is all that I care about. Don't worry, everything will work out."

Telling my father was difficult only because the information was shocking. I could not have imagined a better response. His main concern was about how my husband and I were handling things. He was assured we were working things out in a kind and friendly way. In typical dad form, his concern eventually would be for my finances going forward. The reaction my step mom had when my dad told her was one of the warmest I received. I received a phone call from her the night I told my dad. She said, "Good for you. I am so happy for you and am here for whatever you need. I love you and want you to know I think you are brave and amazing! Please take care of yourself and let us know if you need anything at all." I was two for two so far.

I had a sense when I called my brother it would easily be one of the oddest conversations we'd ever had. We are three years apart in age and most of our bonding as kids came at the expense of my little sister. We may have, on occasion, wrapped her like a burrito in an afghan, each grabbing an end to begin spinning her around like a jump rope. I remember our cutting off chunks of butter from the Tupperware butter dish, coating them in sugar, and generously offering her our twisted version of candy. My brother is a mellow guy and his "I am cool with it" response was a relief. It was all I needed to hear from him to know he was going to be supportive as things unfolded. I was three for three if you are keeping score.

The next on my list was my mom. Telling her was not easy. She is a very devout Catholic and I knew from comments she had made in the past about same sex marriage that she probably was going to have a difficult time with what I was about to unload on her. She told me she loved me anyway and that, while she did not understand the gay thing, she would be praying for us all. It was a short conversation. My sister, who is a fundamentalist Christian, gave me the "you are my sister and I love you anyway" response and I knew that was going to be the extent of support from her. I would later come to find out from a reliable source my mother and sister were not really on board with everything I had shared with them. Three for five was a decent day at the plate.

I shuddered each time I heard the phrase "Well, I love you anyway." It implied there was a problem and communicated there was some kind of flaw in me that needed overlooking. I hate the word "anyway." I had a difficult time accepting people's attempts to be supportive even though the "anyway" was immediately followed by a general wish for my happiness. These were the people who had known me the longest. While I understood the information I shared with them would take time to be fully absorbed, I still cringed when I heard the word "anyway."

As I replayed the reactions of family, I had a revelation about what my parents must have been experiencing as I told them. The latest disclosure from their oldest daughter was a doozy and only added to the character of our family dynamic. They now have a daughter who is a lesbian as well as two divorced children, plus they have dealt with a variety of serious issues among their offspring over the course of their lives. What happened to us happened to them. As a parent, I understand this perfectly. My family is more likely to be compared to a Picasso than to a Normal Rockwell print. This was a glorious thing to realize. None of us are perfect. We will never be. This may seem odd to some, but I believe there is nothing more beautiful than our flaws. Embracing the flawed nature of our lives can be source of joy and the very thing that bonds families together. I have yet to meet a single person who has been spared from having to deal with difficulty, challenges, or adversity in their life. If such a person exists, I am not sure I would want to meet them. My coming out just topped off the cup of interesting in my family.

This first round of reactions gave me a sense about what I could expect as I made my way down the list of those I needed to come out to. I worried the ease at which this went would end up coming back later to bite me in the ass. I was not disappointed. As I continued to make the calls to my friends and extended family, I would hang up the phone and wait for the reactions. In the beginning, there seemed to be initial support and love sent my way. It was only after the shock had worn off that I heard the sound of crickets chirping a little louder than usual. People in general do not like mess. I think some were afraid that my mess was contagious and passed on any involvement.

In my pre-coming out research I had read somewhere I should prepare for the possibility that people's the first reactions may not be a good indicator about how they are really feeling. I thought this meant those who may have reacted badly or negatively in the beginning would eventually come around. I foolishly did not consider the alternative. When I sat down with my two closest friends to tell them, one of them had a very emotional reaction. As we spoke, I was surprised her emotion was exclusively for my husband and children. I felt hurt by this. Of course it was appropriate to be concerned about what they were going through, but I felt invisible. I felt like crawling under the table at the restaurant. It was as if what I was going through did not matter at all. This was the first time I remember thinking I had better get used to this reaction. I was sure it would not be the last time this happened.

Obviously, coming out was a challenge not only for me, but for those in my life. Let's just say that my Christmas card list shrank considerably. Some relationships remained the same after the shock had dissipated, but others changed in ways I still have a difficult time understanding. Relationships are complicated and many of those complications were compounded after I came out. I had expected it on some level but was surprised to discover one of my closest friends and confidants was upset. It took me a year to discover she was angry and I was only tipped off by another friend inadvertently. Again, I had no idea things were not alright with us. I began to wonder if I needed to take a class in knowing when someone is upset with you. My compass seemed to be broken. I learned the upset of the situation and the source of the anger was over five years old and was triggered by my divorce and coming out.

As we spoke, I was able to listen to how she was feeling and understand her perceptions. I was also able to address my part in what had happened and apologize. In the end, it was clear the issue had more to do with her thinking, in light of her own experience, rather than my actions. I wished we could have cleared things up so much earlier and she could have voiced her anger with me when it began. I try to admit when I am wrong and be introspective when it comes to owning my part of a disagreement or situation. I know I am not perfect and make mistakes. I know in order to be healthy, I have to take responsibility for things I've said or did that truly caused pain or hurt to those in my life. I also realize I cannot be responsible for other people's inability to get past their own demons.

I began to see a trend developing as people responded to my coming out. The first thing I noticed was everyone seemed to disclose that they "have one" in their family. Great. I also noticed I suddenly found myself listening to taxicab type confessions from those who had just learned I was a lesbian. A number of people shared with me their stories of their secret same sex experiences. One went so far as to describe their participation in an online porn site. I checked for the "tell me your dirt" sign that someone must have placed on my forehead. I wanted to believe that because I had shared something personal they felt the green light to do likewise. I suspect it had more to do with the overall negative opinion the world holds with regard to homosexuality. I was naïve to be optimistic that they saw a sympathetic soul rather than a deviant one. Many equate being gay with living in a way that is not in alignment with what is believed to be the right way. Instead of being upset and offended, I concluded these conversations were merely a way to relate to one another and a way to reassure ourselves we are not outcasts or deviants.

I noticed many who were close to my wife and I found a way to make what was going on in our lives about them. I called this the "let's make it about me" party. This was my absolute favorite. From the beginning, I maintained that the only people my coming out truly impacted were my husband, my children, and myself. That's it. From what I could tell, knowing that Dawn Waters was a lesbian pretty much had no impact on the daily living of anyone else except those people aforementioned. My being gay did not change or alter anybody else's life directly in any way. I may be crazy, but when something happens to someone in my circle, my daily routines are not affected. Sure, there may be emotions to deal with, but the everyday operations of those not directly involved remain unchanged. I completely understood people needed to make sense of this very shocking development in my life and a measure of reflection upon how this could relate to themselves was to be expected. This is, after all, human nature. We all have a natural tendency to want to figure out how news we hear affects us. It helps us to make sense of things. It is almost a default mindset that kicks in for an instant.

Many times I sat and wondered, in my head and out loud, how the situation I was living could possibly warrant this kind of response. I fully understood and appreciated the mental process those in my life were going through. I never begrudged anyone that reaction. The question I had was if they were feeling this tug and concern about how my situation affected them, why did they feel the need share it with me? I was in no condition to help anyone figure out anything. This was the core of my gripe with those who showed up for the party. People flat out asked me, "how does this affect me?' I cannot even remember what my reply was. At the time, I did not have the energy or desire to explain or express my opinion about how ridiculous I found their question to be. I felt whatever level of personal strife they were experiencing as a result of my homosexuality would be more appropriately dealt with by someone other than me. This is what therapists are for. I had an expectation that instead of asking what I could do for them they should have been asking what they could do for me or my family. This is what I would have done. I have had to understand that not everyone behaves how I would and that this was just one of those things that I had no control over.

The belief that coming out impacted the lives of my immediate family solely was not shared by everyone. I could write an entire book providing illustrations to support this fact. After the shit hit the fan, it was brought to light that my ex's family had never liked me. Ever. A few months before I came out, our family flew across the country to attend one of his family member's wedding. It was a quick trip. While there, I noticed at some point his parents had not spoken a word to me the entire time. We were there for a wedding. It was hectic. We never had any falling outs and I could not think of any one event that would give cause to think something was amiss. As it turns out, they had decided well before I came out that they were not speaking with me. My ex was not even aware they had written me off.

The relationship we had with his family became strained when we decided against marrying in the Catholic Church. His mother was a devout Catholic and refused to attend the wedding. His father respected her wishes so they both declined our invite. I know this upset my husband but, as he saw it, it was their loss and not his. We married and he never told his parents about it. They made it very clear they did not want to know. Four months after we married, his brother got married. My husband travelled to the wedding: I stayed home because I was still bitter about their choice not to be a part of their son's important day. When he went to the airport, he took off his wedding ring and left it at home. I was furious. He did not want to start something with his family that could create stress on his brother's wedding day. I was hurt and somehow knew his decision to play the "hide I am married" game would be something that would end up stinging us both. I understood his reasons but did not accept them. I took his silence as his agreement with their opinion of our marriage. Before he got on the plane to return home, he did manage to tell his mom we were married. She had figured as much.

For years, there was a stink surrounding our wedding. We did not see very much of his family and when we did see them, we always went to wherever they were vacationing. Once we had children, his family would be around for big occasions or birthdays. They would usually leave in the middle of the party, however, and return after everyone else had left. My husband was just as put off and confused by this as I was.

When the levy crashed and I broke their son's heart, one of the reasons they gave was that I was not friendly to them and had never made them feel welcome in my home. I felt like I must have some kind of dissociative personality disorder because that was not at all how I recall acting toward them. They also believed I was a hindrance to their relationship with their son. This was news to me. For years, I tried to do what I could to accommodate them. I would cook dinner and they would show up having already eaten a meal. We figured it was just one of the things they did. They were always at a distance and I now know for sure I was the reason why.

After this information came to light, my ex was angry about this. He took exception and was as confused as I was given that they had never actually said one word or made mention of how they felt about me. Zero discussion. I felt blindsided, but not surprised, by their opinion of me. For something that had been brewing for so long, I was disappointed I was never given the chance to address the things about me they did not like. There was never an opportunity to make right that relationship. Maybe it never could have been any better than it was, but I would have loved the opportunity to see what I could have done to mend whatever needed mending during the twenty years we were a couple.

My ex-husband initially was upset when he learned about their dislike for me. He reacted by choosing not to share any of the details about what was going on in our house with regard to my coming out. In other words, he did not talk to them. One day, he received a scathing email from his father inquiring as to "why he was doing this to his mother after he had not spoken to them" about this. "Her melancholy grows minute by minute…." You get the idea right? It became our jobs to make everyone feel better about this, when in fact we were just surviving what each day would bring. For a long time, there was a high chance that at any given moment someone in our household was crying. There was no rhyme or reason to the emotional waterfalls sprouting from various rooms at any time of the day. As a family, we would have been wise to wear waders as the flood raged. It was a very delicate and raw time for us all, yet we were expected to console everyone else. Again, this was about them right?

Radio silence was short lived. Before I moved out, he tried to plead my case to his family but I don't think any minds were changed. I have not seen nor spoken to them in the four years since our divorce. Eventually my ex and his family agreed to disagree about me and thought that creating a new beginning would be best given that life was too short.

Still Me

I believed I was still Dawn. Being a lesbian was one small part of me. I thought once the initial shock of the situation had worn off many who reacted negatively would circle back because they would realize I was still me. After that first year, it became clear to me how naive I was. I had failed to truly consider other people's opinions about this "lifestyle" I now subscribed to. For some, this is a deal breaker of sorts. I felt very confused by this and wondered what in the hell was going on. I had many individuals who were very supportive, friends and family alike, however, there seemed to be a definite change in a lot of people after this information came to light. I thought long and hard about the reasons and kept coming to a point where was looking around and wondering where everyone went.

I became keenly aware I was now part of a subset of people who live a life not always socially accepted. Conventions dictate if you are a woman married to a man then all is good in the world. Changing this norm unsettled people. I understand most people are uncomfortable with things or situations they do not understand. They have a hard time relating to something that is not what their experience or frame of reference will allow. Social groups are formed based largely upon their commonalities and certain criteria are used to determine who fits in. Basically, this left me feeling like a woman without a country. For years I was identified, and very accepted, as a straight woman who was married to a man. It was a huge part of who I was. Walking down the street hand in hand with him never caused an eyebrow to raise or a head to turn. This was normal. On the day I came out, I no longer fit into the mold. To me, love is love and always has been. When I came out, many people I was very close to just seemed to drop off the earth.

It became very difficult to maintain bonds with those who could not understand this part of my life. I scratched my head because in my mind I was still me. In fact, I was more me than I have ever been. This led me to consider how others might be mourning the loss of the "me" they knew. Acknowledging this has been tough at times, but realizing it was up to me to show those in my life I am still me has been a growing experience. There were many days when I struggled with understanding how my feeling comfortable in my own skin could make those in my life uncomfortable. I just did not get it.

I was floored by the reactions of those same people when the ex-husbands quickly moved on with their lives and found new relationships. My ex was dating before I even moved out of the house. I even had a hand in helping him create his online dating profile. It was my way of min-imizing the damage I was causing. For weeks I witnessed over the top shows of support and happiness for him and his new girlfriend. People could not help themselves. This really drove home the fact that their traditional straight relationship trumped our scandalous lesbian relationship. This was reality and I had a very difficult time coping with it. Things were still very raw and every affirmation of their relationship felt like a dismissal of my own. It hurt. I believed the relationship I was now in warranted just as much positivity and joy as theirs did. I experienced first-hand how straight marriages are viewed in a more legitimate light than same sex relationships. The beauty and depth of my relationship with my wife was never considered or acknowledged by most. I was angry and jealous at the same time. There were many who refused to acknowledge us not only as a couple, but as individu-als.

Some of the most intense interrogation came from those who were hell bent on arguing the morality of my "choice" to be gay. People were uncomfortable with my "choice" to be gay. My choice. To be gay. Imagine the sound of a tea kettle please. Seriously, if you have stayed with me long enough to read up to this point, I ask one question. Who would choose this mess? Let's recap. I felt like I went from hero to zero overnight as I slid down the social ladder. Life changed much more than I thought it would. This can of worms was proving to be more like a silo full of snakes. I hate snakes. I underestimated the amount of time I would have to spend explaining myself to others. I felt like my answers were not sufficient enough to warrant them remaining in my life.

I wondered what else about me made it so easy for people to step back and withdraw? Could it really be just because I was now gay? Were people looking for the chance to bail before this happened and was this the perfect opportunity? Was it me or them? My money was on them. The truth was that I no longer fit into any traditional mold. This time was full of chaos, uncer-tainty, and a strange sense of confusion. Few really understood the difficulty accompanying the situation. I never really felt I needed everyone to completely understand everything during those first few months. The gay bomb overshadowed numerous other changes happening in our lives. I never sought out sympathy, but I certainly would have welcomed some patience and compassion from more than a handful of people. I can count on one hand the number of people who showed genuine concern for how I was doing. I am forever grateful for these people and consider them my angels on this earth.

Adding "the gay" factor was an invitation for criticism, especially by those whose religious beliefs do not support homosexuality. This one element became the eraser of all love in a relationship. One thing. Gay. Relationship changed. This has been my primary struggle. Are people capable of agreeing to disagree about an issue without having the entire relationship become inauthentic? Was it possible for me to still enter in and love despite their objections to my "lifestyle?"

The truth was anything that did not conform to the new fabric of my life was getting tossed in the trash like Clinton and Stacy often did on TLC's *What Not to Wear*. This mindset proved very effective in letting go of those who were outside my inner circle of friends or family. I thought I had done a great job of letting those who expressed some moderate discomfort with my "lifestyle" choose their level of involvement with me. I realized, however, some very important relationships were existing in limbo. I am not a fan of things being out in the wind. I wanted definitive status reports. For as free as I felt, I still needed to make sure my emotional ground was as stable as it could be. I felt like a baby being thrown out with the rainbow colored bath water so I tried to beat them to it. I struggled with how this one part of me could warrant an overall rejection of my whole person.

In the early days of "gay Dawn," I was very insistent that anyone who did not like this could lump it. Part of my decision to be this way came from not wanting to have dissenters in my camp as I moved forward. The other part came about as a way to protect myself from the pain I was feeling. There was enough to deal with in my daily life and frankly I did not need the aggravation. As I navigated the new terrain of my life, I didn't feel the need to maintain contact with those who were not supportive or took issue with "the gay thing" or "the lifestyle." Who needs that? Nope, not me, not interested. I am not interested in debating my "choice" to be gay with anyone or engaging in circular arguments with those who may never change their mind about homosexuality.

I did not have any contact with one very dear family member for a number of years after I was out. This particular person had been in my life since I was born and we were very close up until I came out. I felt like gay Pigpen from the Peanuts Gang. I was still so raw from everything that my delay in straightening shit out was my own version of "don't ask, don't tell." What I did not know couldn't hurt me, until not knowing started to hurt more. I needed to protect myself from the possibility of being hurt by those closest to me, but I could not shake the feeling I had unfinished business to tend to with her. There was a tension and separation that could not be ignored. By reaching out, I had to be prepared for whichever way the conversation played out.

I picked up the phone and just flat out asked how she felt about me. I shared my feelings about not having any contact for so long. During the course of the phone call, I learned her radio silence was related to her assumption I would not be respectful or accepting of her position about gay marriage and homosexuality. If I have learned anything over the last three years, it is that without respect there can be no love, progress, or understanding. These ideas are central to my thinking and, in order for me to be truly authentic, I have to extend these same things to others who do not share my worldview. I believe this is the key to civility and maintaining peace in my world. I have become much more tolerant and patient with those who present objections, for whatever reason, because I realize many are afraid of what they do not understand.

I believe love is fearless. If I am going to practice what I preach to my kids each day then I have to resist being afraid of what or who might leave my life. Fear is a powerful and destructive relationship killer. When I entered back into this relationship that had been hanging in suspended animation for three years, I was mindful of the emotional risk I would be taking. In the end, the risk was worth the reward because a new starting point was born out of that one conversation. I am glad I did not dismiss this relationship because it would have resulted in more damage and prevented opportunities for healing for us both.

CHAPTER 7

Out in the Open

I am a fan of getting people together.

— *Ellen DeGeneres*

Life did not stop because I came out. I honestly do not know how the hell I got to here from there those first few months. My putting one foot in front of the other created an impression for some that everything was fine with me and I was just going to grab my flannel shirt, jump in my jeep, and drive roughshod into my new life. I was offended that the people who professed to know me best could possibly think that this situation would not have a huge impact on me. I admit, I experienced moments of anger and bitterness when I felt invisible. I was emotionally wrecked and was trying to keep it all together. I know others saw a peace about me after I came out. On the outside, I seemed calm and matter of fact about everything. On the inside, however, I had so much going beneath my game face. I was running back and forth trying to keep all of the plates spinning. I needed to find a way to step out of the isolation I was feeling. I needed to reframe my thinking and begin to look past the pile of emotional debris I was buried under. I needed to step up to the plate and to grow thicker skin.

Think about the most private and personal thing you have ever experienced in your life. Now visualize sitting down at the computer and writing it all down. Then ponder opening up Facebook, copying what you have written, and making it your status post. The entire public was the audience. Think about what it would feel like to share the intimate details of that situation. Would you do it? You might if you thought you could help someone in some way. This is what writing my blog felt like.

I was nervous about divulging the gritty details of my life and exposing myself to criticism or inviting conflict from others. I knew there would always be the possibility of someone sharing their objections to my "choices" if I did. I was hesitant and my heart was pounding the first time I put my words out there for the world to see. I even had a moment of "what the hell did I just do?" when I hit post for the very first time. My motivation for sharing the intimate and often mundane details of this period in my life was strictly for my own therapy and healing. I had a choice to make. I could do something positive with all of this or stay safely cocooned within the four walls of my house licking my wounds. I knew if I started to let the details trickle out to the world it could result in a disaster of epic proportions that might run me out of town. Ever read the Scarlet Letter? I also realized there was an opportunity for someone reading about my experience to come to a new understanding in their view of homosexuality. I had to find a way to show those who hated, were confused, or just ignorant about gay people that homosexuals are humans, just like them.

Did I mention that at times I have been naïve through this process? I decided being negative was counterproductive. Instead, I was going to remain optimistic about people and their ability to change how they think, feel, or act towards those different from themselves. I felt the best way to do this was to begin a blog about my experience. I offered front row seats to any who were curious about what going through this was like. After writing my first few posts, I frequently checked the hit counter on the website and was surprised to see people were actually visiting the site. I didn't know who they were, but I hoped in some way my sharing would help them understand what a mile in my shoes felt like.

Through the glory of social media, I began to share my blog on my Facebook and Twitter feeds. I would check to see if my friend's lists on these sites were plummeting. I was glad to discover the number dropped by only a few. This avenue was a safe way for someone to peek into the window of our house and see what was really going on. If what I wrote could soften someone's heart in the process it would be an added bonus. I was shocked when, after three months, I noticed a new message in my inbox on Facebook. It was from a friend from high school. I knew from many of her posts she was a devout Christian and a very godly woman. My first reaction was fear. I was afraid of what might be waiting for me when I opened the message. Back in those early days, I was gun shy and mildly paranoid.

To my surprise, it was a very touching and heartfelt message I will never forget. She shared her experience as a child of a parent who came out when she was in her late teens. Presenting my perspective really hit home as she read about what it must have been like for her parent to go through the same experience I did. I felt such joy and peace after reading her personal story and appreciated her positive and encouraging words to me regarding my kids and her wishes for my happiness. I felt blessed and grateful she had the courage to share something so personal with me and will always remember how reading those kind words made me feel during that rocky time. This was the first of many times someone reached out to me and thanked me for writing. Knowing my words helped put a face on the subject of coming out later in life motivated me to continue blogging. It was a wonderful validation of both my decisions to live openly and authentically as a gay woman and to share the details with the world.

I received another message along those same lines right before my wife and I were about to jaunt off and get married. From the very beginning, we chose to be open and share our lives with the world. This included our excitement about our wedding. The message speaks for itself.

Reader: *I know you don't know me very well, and you only know me as an extension through someone else, but I want you to know that you have had a tremendous impact on me personally and that your blog has brought so much insight, confusion, compassion, understanding, and love to me. I just wanted to thank you and wish you a wonderful wedding.*

My reply: *I am so happy to hear that. This is why I do this. I am glad that it has had a positive effect on you. I appreciate your telling me so. Thanks for the good wishes!*

Reader: *It has had more than a positive effect on me, but also a positive effect on those close to me, that I had had such a difficult time understanding. Thank you for being brave enough to share your journey."*

This feedback was healing not only for the people who commented, but also for me. I was often annoyed when I heard stories about how staunch critics of gays suddenly stopped hating them when someone close to them came out. I found it very difficult to stomach the "Saul getting knocked off his horse on the way to Damascus" experience. Saul changed his mind about persecuting Christians when he was blinded by the light of Jesus. His heart changed in one instant. How was it so easy for those who had previously been so vocal and hateful towards homosexuals to change their mind? It seemed so disingenuous. I felt like it was dismissive and convenient for them to now pick up the rainbow flag and start waving it.

My reaction to this was very strong in the beginning. I had a hard time understanding how such deep opposition could melt away in an instant. Then I realized my negative reaction was rooted in my own anger and hurt regarding those who seemed to disappear from my life when I came out. I was reminded God knocked Saul off of that horse and facilitated that conversion. It happened in an instant. I had forgotten God works in mysterious ways. I got knocked off of my horse of judgment just as quickly as they had changed their views on gays. I was also reminded the final score was more important than what happened in the batting cages during warm ups. The truth is for some it takes having a loved one come out for them to reach a place of understanding and acceptance. There are few things more powerful than the impact a personal experience can have in changing someone's heart.

CHAPTER 8

Rebel with a New Cause

One's philosophy is not best expressed in words; it is expressed in the choices one makes...and the choices we make are ultimately our responsibility.

— *Eleanor Roosevelt*

When I came out, I was ready to move forward, but felt stuck. I looked around and saw daily life looked a lot like it did before I left my other house, except without the financial security I once had enjoyed. I was ready to take on the world and be amazing. I was ready to accept whatever that looked like. I wanted to pursue opportunities I knew were in my wheelhouse and explore the possibilities that would bring me some personal satisfaction. I had a small voice in my head telling me my life up until that point had been a waste of time. I told her to shut up. I understood everything I had experienced was an important part of preparing me for my future. I knew my prospects, however, I could not figure out how to pursue them given the responsibilities I still had to my kids. I was being financially supported by my ex-husband via child support and alimony, and I struggled knowing I was not generating my own income yet. I wanted to be responsible for myself financially, which was something I had never really achieved in the past.

The mystery of my sexuality had been solved, however, solving the mystery of what my life was going to look like had just begun. I was in a holding pattern and was unsure how to get moving forward. The majority of choices I made in the past were rooted in some kind of fear or anxiety. I would have instances where I felt like I could do anything I set my mind to. I would make plans, but fear always seemed to have the last word and convince me the safe route would be the better route to take. With age comes wisdom and certain degree of not giving a fuck. I am proud to report that my fearless choices are slowly outnumbering my safe ones. I have taken on challenges that I never imagined. I have opened two businesses and have written a book. I have learned that becoming fearless is a process that can be frustrating and often follows a two steps forward, three steps back pattern.

My frustration with everyday life reared its ugly head about a year after everything blew up. I tried so hard to minimize the impact of being gay that the more I tried to mitigate the circumstance the more resentful I grew. Each day I was just trying to do the right thing. The irony was that I kept doing the right thing for everyone but myself. I found myself mentally right back to where I had been for so many years when the "I am not important" tape played on repeat in my ears. It was mutually agreed upon I would continue to stay at home for the kids. We thought this would be the best way to ease the transition for everyone. My story was still being written by everyone else. I wanted to flex my new self-awareness muscles and freely move about the cabin. I was tired of fear driving my car and letting my life be dictated by what everyone else needed.

I have been accused of being a rebel. I cannot disagree with this assessment because of some of the choices I have made in the past. From an early age, I was never satisfied just blending in and being quiet. In addition to the nickname of Demon Dawn, my parents also referred to me as "The Mouth" or on days when I was being especially obnoxious just "Mouth" (which was most often said through clenched teeth). As I made my way through the angsty teen years, my failure to shut up was problematic. Mainly for my lips. Ninety nine percent of my fat lip incidents can be attributed to the fact that I chose moments when riding in the front seat of the car with my mom to start popping off. I would usually be at my mouthiest in route to help my mom clean offices in the evenings while in middle school. I was not exactly thrilled to be dragged along on these adventures and, being I was dumb, I would offer nothing in the way of positive conversation the entire way there. By the time we had finished cleaning, I was smelly, sweaty, and just plain over it. I really amped it up on the ride home. My indignation would get completely ridiculous and boom, pop to the mouth. I never learned being restrained by a seat belt only inches from the backhand was not a great plan.

For someone who thought she knew everything, I did not learn the inherent stupidity of this. I had it coming. I admit it. The memory of these occasions is precisely why I thank God every day for blessing me with boys so I have never had to suffer at the hands of the kind of teen aged daughter I was. My dad knew what went down when the front door opened and my lip entered before I did. He would just shake his head and remark, "Popped off again, huh?" I still remember the way their voices sounded as they discussed why I just would not knock off the mouth as I climbed the stairs to my room. I was a rebel with absolutely no cause, and poor timing.

One way I tried to reconnect with my inner rebel after I came out was to figure out what new "me" looked like. I needed a makeover representative of my authentic self. I began the process of weeding out what I should keep and what should go. I needed to get this right. You only come out once and I wanted to make an impression. The freedom I now had to express myself was overwhelming at times. My application of that freedom often gave way to what some would consider rebellious decisions. I spent time considering every detail of my life. My clothes, my "look," and even the way others saw me had to be evaluated. Not analyzing these things just would not be who I was. When I was able to take the time I needed to imagine what my life could look like, I would get excited. I had ideas of what "lesbian me" should look like. I was just learning how to move around without all of the chains that had bound up my self-image in the past. I did not undergo a drastic change; little expressions of who I was were important as I embraced my new path. I tossed the gold jewelry to the side and discovered I preferred stainless steel and silver things. I wore rings on fingers other than my ring fingers. I bought a big chunky watch and stocked my closet with Converse low tops.

My relationship with athletic footwear would have made Imelda Marcos proud. I love me some sneakers that is for sure. Being confident in myself meant I could explore things just for exploration sake where wardrobe and footwear was concerned. This may sound silly, but it was a big deal to me at the time. My wife and I experienced our first ladies' night at a local gay bar and thought we had died and gone to heaven. We were surrounded by people like us, which was something we were not used to. Our life was now the exception rather than the rule, however, we felt normal when we were there. We felt accepted and welcome. It was something we desperately wanted to experience but did not know how important it would end up being until we actually got in the car and went. As fun as shopping for clunky jewelry and sneakers was, I was surprised by how difficult it became to stay rooted in the peace coming out had brought. I could dress like a lesbian and shop all day long, but I still felt the weight of figuring out how to create a life apart from what I had known in the past. I was shocked to discover my inner rebel had been hijacked long ago. It was clear I was going to have to find a way regain control of the plane and level my wings.

After forty years, I had come to the place where I felt fearless and really wanted to get out there. I have never been a "grass is always greener" type of thinker. I did not for a single instant believe the solution to every issue I'd ever faced would be handed to me on a silver plate and my life would be perfect just because I came out. Yet, for the first time, I felt the grass under my feet was green as the grass on the other side of the fence. I wanted the opportunity to decide for myself where I lived or what I did for a living. I needed to make up for lost time and could not afford to spend another moment in limbo. While I was determined to figure out my next steps, my options seemed limited.

I knew the path ahead of me would be challenging but I was confident everything would be alright. I had a new optimism about life, but there were times I found myself feeling lost and alone. My optimism wasn't enough to overcome my desire to not shake up things any more than I already had. I needed to bring in some income, but believed I had no right to enact any more drastic changes in the kids' lives. I had done enough damage. Leaving my children to enter the workforce would have been devastating to them. My youngest son would become very upset when my working outside of the home was mentioned. I was all about the kids.

Underneath my good intentions and pure motives, I was hurting myself. I was growing resentful and depressed. My anxiety level was again rising and I was fighting it the whole time, which only made it worse. I tried to squash the thought I was going back to the place of darkness I had felt before I came out. It was hard to know what I was supposed to do. I felt pulled in every direction imaginable. I knew I needed to do what I needed to do for me and it felt so selfish. Hadn't I been selfish enough?

It was time to choose me. I wasn't sure what that would look like. I was sick and tired of feeling so awful about the pain my family had endured because I was gay. I had to choose what was going to be good for me for once. Exercising this freedom is hard, especially for a mom. Changing up the normal flow of life often makes people uncomfortable. Boundaries are redrawn and shifting the line between where someone else begins and another ends can cause confusion and hurt feelings. It is never easy to say to someone, "I choose me and it has nothing to do with you," without seeming cold, insensitive, and selfish. After some encouragement from my wife, I embarked on an official job search. Staying at home with my children had left a gap in my work history. I had participated in many activities and organizations during those years at home, but translating my skill set to potential employers was a challenge.

Choices

When I got pregnant, it was decided that I would be a stay-at-home mother. This was a perfect arrangement for me. My levels of anxiety were so high and the idea of hanging out in my cave for the great calling of motherhood was something I really looked forward to. This would allow my husband to do what he needed to do for his career and life would be consistent for our kids. The time after my first son was born was the most peaceful time in my life. He was an easy baby and I was thankful I had those moments with him as I began my journey as a mom. Fast forward and add another two sons to the mix and life got hectic. My days were consumed with housework, errands, kids, and all of the things that go along with being the CEO of a family of five. I was the chief financial officer as well as the plant manager. I was social coordinator and culinary director. I was the chauffeur, nurse, and live-in maid. In addition to all of these roles, I was very involved with my church community and enjoyed many opportunities to be in leadership positions and ministries. The outlets I chose were things that fit into the family routine given my constraints as a woman with three children. These experiences kept me sane and gave me the sense I was contributing outside of the house. I loved being at home with the kids, but there were times I thought I was missing out on what was happening out in the world.

I always felt there was so much I wanted to accomplish separate from my motherhood status. There just never seemed to be a good time to make this happen. On particularly difficult days, I would find myself thinking that going to college had been a waste of time because my daily grind was hardly something one needed a higher education to perform. It is very natural for women to get lost in the business of raising children. Many of my friends who were also at home with their children experienced the same thoughts. This was a 24 hour a day job and, while there were many benefits, sometimes it just felt monotonous. Children are a blessing and I am so grateful for my family, but I felt being a stay-at-home mom was not my only calling. Being a mom is one part of who I am and what I do. God created us as multidimensional beings, capable of many things.

After I came out, I found myself laser focused on my limitations. It was not pretty. I was an angry elf and disagreeable to anyone who tried to point out the good things all around me. Whichever way I looked, I could only see the things that were not options for me. I realized one day this was making me, and everyone I lived with, miserable. I needed to knock this shit off. I had to stop dwelling on things I could not change and force myself to only think about areas I could do something about. I couldn't change the gap in my work history or that I still had children to raise. I could not change my physical location nor could I change what other people thought about this whole situation. Feeling stuck, however, was something I could change. In the midst of my "poor me" thinking, I had forgotten one of my go to mantras in life —if you can't change your situation, change your attitude.

In college, I was selected to be a resident advisor on campus housing. My motivation for applying for this position was strictly financial. Resident advisors had their rooms paid for. As part of residential life training, we were required to become well versed in campus rules, proper incident reporting procedures, planning fun activities for the residence hall, and how to deal with students in a variety of ways. We were taught proper protocol for handling emotional situations with our residents and role played situations which ranged from finding an illegal cooking device to how to handle being woken up in the middle of the night to deal with a suicidal resident. We were an eclectic group of college students who thought we already had more wisdom than most simply by virtue of being chosen to be part of the staff.

We were also an egotistical group. We were full of ourselves and a little drunk with power over our new leadership roles. For most of us, the training was a social event and we all had a good time that week. I was expecting to learn many things and I was not disappointed. I took something away, however, from that week of staff performances and late night antics in the empty halls that I didn't realize would have such a deep impact on my thinking and formation of my world view. The director of the program, who was a mentor to me, shared this simple quote with the group: "If you can't change your situation, change your attitude." For some reason, this stuck with me. I had never heard this before and its simplicity caught my attention.

This statement was the most profound thing I heard that day while crammed into a sweltering lecture hall. My kids know this concept better than they care to. I have long seen the choreographed eye rolls from my boys as they too have been indoctrinated into this way of looking at the world. It is their least favorite lecture because the lesson requires action on their part. This straightforward phrase reminds them they are in control of their thinking as well as whatever situation they find themselves in. The freedom to change thinking is obvious, but it is the freedom to change situations I did not fully realize until much later in my life.

Changing thinking takes time and a great degree of patience. I began to readjust my attitude and it occurred to me what I was lacking was patience. I knew it would take time to start over but I could hear the ticks of my chronological clock as the remaining moments of my life passed. At times, I panicked thinking I did not have much life left and I did not want to waste another minute of it. I know that sounds a little dramatic, but this thought would tighten my chest and make it difficult to breathe. I was chomping at the bit. Patience and moderation are not my natural state of existence. I have the tendency to be black or white with my thinking, which I have worked on a lot over the years.

When I was a wellness coach, I continuously preached to my clients that within them was the ability to make life look any way they chose. I reminded them nothing that was worth anything was easy. I explained feeling uncomfortable was a necessary part of the growth process and key to their meeting goals or feeling peace in their lives. As I moved forward, I recognized avoiding discomfort did not change any circumstances but hindered my own growth.

I am reminded on a daily basis I am an impatient person. I believe the lesson of patience is going to be on the syllabus of my life forever. I know my impatience creates opportunities for me to become more patient. I never pray for patience. Ever. Praying for patience is a sure fire way to find yourself knee deep in opportunities to practice being patient. I learned that lesson many years ago. I had to understand that in order to create a meaningful life I was going to have to learn how to sit and wait for things to unfold.

Even with my continued efforts to remember most of life happens in the gray areas, I still get tripped up in black and white thinking. I had many moments of being torn between the idea of my right to be happy and my responsibility to other people, especially my family. My logic after coming out was since I had caused this, I had to sacrifice my own happiness for the sake of everyone else. This was an equally impossible and unrealistic task to take on. We can only be responsible for our own happiness. Operating out of guilt was like trying to swim across the Atlantic Ocean with cinder blocks attached to my feet. I had to let it go.

CHAPTER 9

Full Disclosure

*If I do a good job, people won't care
if I am green or have three heads.*

— *Harvey Milk*

I chose to live openly as a lesbian from day one. As I began my job search, I had to consider the implications this could have on my ability to earn a living. Fortunately, this is not something the majority of people have to think about before they head out the door in the morning. If you are not gay, you may not think this is a big deal. For those who are members of this unprotected class of workers, it assuredly is. In the state I live in, it is perfectly legal to fire someone because they are LGBTQ. There are currently no protections in place to stop an employer from removing a person from their position simply because she is gay. There are many homosexual employees who hide their sexual orientation from their employers. Many groups are lobbying for changes to this current policy, but until the laws are changed it is a risk every LGBTQ person assumes the moment they accept a new job or are outed at their current job. Because I have been open about my sexuality from the beginning, I am only a google search away from my sexual orientation being discovered by a prospective employer. Google is often the first step taken by employers vetting job applicants. I know it is for me. If anyone lands on my Facebook page, within seconds they will notice my relationship status and that I am a woman married to another woman.

The fear of being fired or not being hired in the first place are legitimate concerns for members of the gay community. Think about it. It becomes serious business when someone's ability to financially provide for themselves or their families is involved. Some will say "just get a new job" if your employer is not gay friendly. Most employers do not advertise this policy so, while a lovely idea, it is unrealistic to expect that this will solve the problem. Imagine a work day where you couldn't mention your partner or spouse without giving away your sexual orientation. There is a burden involved with having to censor what you say or what pictures you have on your desk. Even having a typical Monday morning water cooler conversation with someone who asks about your weekend can lead to disaster if you are not careful. Of course, many work places do not discriminate, but until you get in you never really know what the situation may be. If you ask during an interview if the company is gay friendly, the answer may be yes on paper, but in practice that may not be the case. All it takes is one homophobic manager or coworker to upset the apple cart. If you do not mention it at the interview and end up getting hired, you have to proceed with caution until you get the lay of the land. Not being able to freely be who you are is an unfair burden in any circumstance, gay or straight. All this was yet another new layer added to my life. I would need to tread carefully as I continued to move forward.

My first job search in years became another lesson in patience. I had put together a functional resume because my work experience was years old and the title of stay-at-home mom wasn't dropping the jaws of potential employers. I seemed to have more success with jobs I found posted on craigslist. The first job interview I landed was with a local company who manufactured auto parts. It was a family owned and operated business that had posted an opening for a full-time administrative assistant position. The pay was excellent for the area and I agreed to come in for an interview. This was my first interview in seventeen years. I was very nervous and just wanted to get through it without puking on the desk. I was confident in my ability to do the job as it was described to me during our initial pre-interview conversation, but I was terrified any small talk might out me. I left the interview not knowing whether or not I would get the job based on my weak resume. I figured if I did get hired it was most likely because I did a great job of hiding how terrified I was or that they were desperate to fill the position with a warm body.

A few days later, I was offered employment. I accepted and began what would end up holding the record for my second shortest stint with an employer. I was with the company for a total of three weeks. During my interview, the owner of the auto part company explained the job had a very big learning curve. He said it would take a few months for me to get the hang of things. I specifically asked because I was concerned that I was a bit rusty and I wanted to reassure myself I would have time to get back into the work groove if I was hired. What he said and what transpired turned out to be two different things.

I arrived at the aluminum sided building and stepped into a time machine. The office looked like a 1960's paneled cave. My stapler literally looked like the first one ever produced. Next, I was introduced to the guys in the warehouse. When I say guys in the warehouse, I mean all 50 or so of them. All were big, burly mechanic types with gun racks in their trucks and every single one of them spoke with a thick southern drawl. I recall seeing a few confederate flags hanging from their trucks as they pulled in. The physical environment of the office took some getting used to. When I stepped through the front door each morning, I was in good ole boy land. I took photos to show my family so they would believe what I was telling them. They can confirm I am not exaggerating.

I was one of two women in the entire outfit. The other was a blonde accounting assistant who hid in the back office all day. I was at the front desk and right in the middle of everything. One of the few perks of this job was the two of us had our own restroom, which, had this not been the case, I would have been out of there the first day. I live with three young males who share a bathroom and know the kind of mess they are capable of producing. I can only imagine what the restroom in the warehouse looked like.

My work duties included taking orders for engine parts and handling all of the shipping and coding for the orders. I may have not been in an office setting for a long time, but it was obvious to me the internal system I needed to learn was one of the most ass backward I had ever seen. There were pages and pages of procedures to learn for each separate vendor. There were lists of unit numbers that stretched from the ceiling to the floor. I am a fast study, but this was a training by fire situation. I screwed up hourly. I botched uploads to the shipping sites and spent a good portion of my first few days apologizing to customers for the long holds they experienced as I tried to locate part numbers and prices from the great wall of auto parts. The person responsible for training me sat next to me. He watched over my shoulder and huffed each time I forgot to fill in a required field. A few times he just pushed my chair aside and did it himself. It was an interesting first week. The only reason I didn't quit then was because the manager had told me that the learning curve was huge. I figured I would get it eventually. I am good with computers, but this was absolutely unbelievable.

As the second week came around, the huffy guy babysitting me decided he wanted to chit chat about his family. I politely nodded and kept my mouth shut as he talked about his conservative Christian upbringing and the fact that his father was a preacher. Perfect. His chatter wasn't helping me to do any better than I did the week before. I found it weird he was so interested in getting to know the dumb ass who could not do anything right. I'm fairly certain he checked me out on Facebook and discovered I was a lesbian. At the time I drove a Jeep Commander. Yes, a Jeep. He mentioned "a girl I knew in college who was gay had one of those." I knew at that moment he was fishing. Two could play at that game. I cast my net by asking him if he was married, hoping he would ask me the same. He did. I replied I was divorced and in a wonderful relationship with a woman. He outwardly indicated "that was cool" but I sensed an immediate shift. After our conversation ended, he decided he would leave me on my own to figure things out. By the end of the second week, I had fewer mistakes under my belt and I was overjoyed my performance was improving.

The third week began and I could tell my time there would be shorter than I expected. On day two of my third week, the trainer called me into his office an hour before quitting time and said, "You are not progressing as I had hoped and you really need to get on the ball." I had been there for 12 days. I reminded him the owner had told me there was a significant learning curve and I expressed my confusion about the situation. I could not believe this guy was serious.

I returned the next day and received another lecture about how I had not caught on quickly enough and how he was concerned with my progress. He seemed more hostile than the day before which made me feel like crawling under a rock. With every sentence I felt more and more inept and like a complete loser. He again had waited until an hour before quitting time to speak to me. I sat and watched the clock creep along until I could punch my card and get the hell out of there. I ugly cried the whole way home. I felt humiliated because I wanted to be successful at going back to work. This was a giant step for me and I had failed miserably. True, I was struggling and was not on my A game. I also knew I would have caught on. I am stubborn and really get fired up when people question my ability to do something. Being told that I can't do something is an invitation to prove someone wrong. This time, instead of getting motivated, I quit and never went back.

When I called the following morning and quit, I received no argument or apologies from the owner who hired me. In an attempt to save my last shred of dignity, I called him out about the fact what he told me about the learning curve was not truthful. I suggested he consider a more accurate presentation of the job and its difficulty level when he began interviewing for the position. I had to have the last word. He apologized for the misunderstanding and let me know he would be happy to provide a reference for any other jobs I might apply for. I thought this was very odd given I was told by his right hand man I was completely inept and going to bankrupt the company with my continuous mistakes.

There is no question in my mind if I had chosen to stay for the duration of my 90 day probationary period they would have let me go at the end of it. That man was on a mission to get me out of there based on the rising level of hostility accompanying each conversation. I would bet my last nickel the gay chick was not someone they wanted to work with. Of course nothing was directly said, but I was not an idiot. This was just not the place for me and I quickly rallied once I got another few bouts of ugly crying out of the way.

In retrospect, there were many reasons why this job did not pan out. My mistakes definitely contributed to my departure, but I believe my sexual orientation sped up the inevitable. My biggest mistake was letting my fear about being open with my sexual orientation from the beginning take center stage. Tiptoeing around this created a conflict within myself and made me feel inauthentic. I was determined to never let this happen again.

After this disappointing experience, I reaffirmed my desire to find something I could do where I could work for myself. I was able to find some part-time house cleaning gigs which brought in a few dollars each week. I was fortunate to meet a wonderful family who treated me very well during my employment. Near the end of my time with them, I began to seriously consider becoming a certified personal trainer. In my former life before children, my background had been in fitness, I believed returning to this area of expertise would be a great way to earn money.

Personal training was something I had done at a number of fitness facilities. I had great experiences working with people who were trying to reach their wellness goals. My undergraduate degree was in sports administration but I was never certified as a trainer. I passed the ASCM Certified

Personal Trainer exam in April of 2012 and began accepting clients. I had a fairly strong response from people in my inner circle and my wellness coaching business was born. I hoped it would be a way to bring in the money we needed, but for many reasons it did not create the amount of income I had envisioned. I enjoyed working with my clients and watching them transform not only their bodies but their thinking as they went through the eight week program I designed. There also was a freedom I felt working for myself. I would never have to deal with my sexuality in a work place setting as long as I was self-employed.

In January of 2013, I interviewed for a personal trainer position in a chiropractic office. I did not want a repeat of what had happened at the auto part factory and decided to get in front of things right from the start. At the end of my interview and facility tour, I volunteered I was a lesbian and wanted to know if this was going to be a problem if I was hired. The risk in giving full disclosure was much less stressful than going to work each day wondering when someone was going to find about me. I needed to be open about this part of me if I was going to do my absolute best at this job. My ability to perform the job had nothing to do with my sexual orientation of course, but it was important to me my co-workers knew who I was.

This was an amazing job. I worked part-time and the schedule was ideal. I worked with many amazing individuals in a variety of ways. Some patients were rehabbing injuries and others were personal training clients working toward weight loss goals. I kept this job for five months. I miss the great people I met at this office. I feel blessed and fortunate this positive experience helped diminish the lingering negative feelings from the auto part job. I left the position because I was ready to activate my five year old sales associate license and pursue real estate full-time. I still had a long way to go to earn the amount of money needed to support a family. The part-time income helped but it just was not enough.

I first was licensed in 2007. I found a broker to park my license under, but I didn't have any intention of getting the ball rolling at that time. Each time my license was up for renewal, I vacillated about what possessed me to do this in the first place and berated myself for wasted time since I did not sell any homes. For years, I would beat myself up for never finishing anything I started. Getting a real estate license was yet another thing I had worked toward but never did anything with. For some reason, though, I could never bring myself to let it lapse. I kept up with all of my continuing education requirements and renewals over the years because it is a difficult license to obtain. I did not want the hard work put in to go down the drain. In 2009, I placed my license in voluntary inactive status and it stayed that way until spring of 2013.

The timing of my leaving the chiropractor office coincided with the recovery of real estate market from the crash that happened a few years earlier. It was time to dust off the license and make a real go at it. I was determined to find a way to bring consistent income into our household. I was relentless. I called my old broker, told him I was coming on board, and was interested in doing this full time. I realized very quickly the importance of timing. I had thought this particular endeavor was just one of the things I did to fill my time. A task I could complete that would help give me some sense of value back when I was trying to find a way to feel important. As it turns out, getting this license and keeping it up to date was one of the best decisions I ever made. I am certain if I had a crystal ball back in 2007 I never would have believed what the future would hold.

To be a successful Realtor, it's necessary to call upon and grow a strong sphere of influence for referrals and customers. In simple terms, this means friends, family, and their friends and family. When I came out, my potential sphere of influence shrank considerably. The scandal of the situation caused many to drop off the face of the earth. This presented yet another challenge as I began to market myself as a real estate agent to friends and past acquaintances. I was known as a mom and the chick who did church stuff. Hardly a credible sales pitch to anyone who wanted to buy or sell a home. I needed to brand myself and spread the word I was a real estate agent. Another new adventure to add to the list of changes. My name was no longer what it was when I was married and many who knew me prior to this were still referring to me by my previous name, including my broker. I straightened that out really quickly.

For as many people who would not enlist my services even if I was the last real estate agent on the planet, I hoped there were just as many who knew nothing of my past that I could create new connections with. I had to convince myself there were at least a few who had escaped the sordid story of the chick who ran off with her best friend. My living in a smallish town did not help. I met with my broker often when I first started and looked to him for guidance about whether or not my being gay would be an obstacle to overcome in this career. I was hyper focused on figuring out how to best sell myself as an agent. I did not want to lose any potential customers if they knew I was gay yet I also did not want to be in the closet.

I struggled with this conflict frequently in the beginning. So many changes were happening I could not control and I wanted to find one I could control. I focused on the information about my sexual orientation. The best advice my broker gave me was to be me. If someone didn't want to work with me because I was gay, so be it. He told me if I was not me then I wouldn't be successful. The most important elements of a professional real estate agent are knowledge, expertise, customer service, and the ability to be genuine and honest with every client. He told me I probably didn't want to work with someone who had an issue with my being gay. He also cautioned me against trying to be someone I am not just to get a listing or a new buyer.

I had known my broker for many years and we always had a very good relationship. I am grateful for the wisdom he gave me in the beginning stages of my real estate career. I did heed his advice and, as it turns out, I am really great at this job. I found something I love doing. Failing was never an option and I learned there is nothing more motivating than sheer necessity. I am an independent contractor and at the end of every listing appointment I let the potential seller know I am gay. A listing appointment is the time where the agent and seller decide if the relationship is going to be something they are interested in proceeding with. I give sellers the opportunity to decide if my being a lesbian is a deal breaker. I have yet to encounter one client who has declined my services after hearing my listing presentation and my plan for selling their home for top dollar. The day I do, I will graciously thank them for their time and wish them the best with their home sale. Then, I will move on to the next one.

CHAPTER 10

Wearing the Pants

I have not failed. I've just found 10,000 ways
that won't work.

— *Thomas Edison*

I

t seemed things were finally settling down and life had normalized. The chaos was waning and most days I was emotionally content. On those days if I could have put how I was feeling into a pill and bottled it I would have. Sprinkled in to the mix was also the struggle I felt about figuring out how to be on my own for the first time in my life. Those pills would have come in handy on the days where I realized I was just starting life for the first time, not necessarily starting over. For years, I had relinquished any say in how my life had turned out. I had made decisions based out of fear and deferred to living a safe and "kept" life. I can say with absolute certainty coming out was the first decision I made in life that was fearless.

The path I took was the direct result of my inability to trust in myself and what I was capable of doing. Taking a trip in the way back machine was never my favorite thing to do but I had to in order to move forward. Every choice I made brought me to where I am today. The good ones, the bad ones, and the downright stupid ones. When the student is ready, the teacher appears and usually at the worst possible moment. I understand the journey has been uniquely mine and I feel gratitude most days. There are also days, though, where I cannot seem to cheer myself past the obstacles I see on the horizon. While grateful for these lessons, I couldn't help feeling pissed off about how long they took to learn and the price I paid from being so slow on the uptake.

The calculated decisions I made early in my adult life were my enemy as I moved forward after coming out. I regretted not establishing a career of my own right out of the gate and relying upon others to provide for me financially. Hindsight has been my constant companion in the years since I've come out. I decided against pursuing a graduate degree in athletic training at an out of state school and instead got married the year after I graduated from college. I chose to stay at home with my children when they were born. Logically, I know I can't go back and change any of the decisions I've made. I have said "if only" more times than I care to admit and have spent countless hours in therapy working my way out of this thought garbage can. Finances is one area this "if only" thinking has really been difficult to reconcile. Specifically, the lack of my own.

Finances are the ugly step sister for most adults. As a married woman, I managed the household finances and handled the bills. Before my ex and I married, we both had jobs and managed to make enough to meet the bills while he was finishing his Master's degree. It was tight in the beginning as he was just starting the climb up the corporate ladder. In our first four years of marriage, we moved four times. The first two were transfers with the same company and the last two were long distance. In those early years, I worked part-time depending on where we were living and what I could find.

He worked full time for a telecom and on the weekend worked at a bowling alley to make ends meet. Eventually he accepted a position in the northeast with another telecom company with the goal of increasing his salary. We stayed just under a year and then he accepted a position back in Florida with yet another company. During the fourth move, I was pregnant with our first child. We collectively decided he would be the bread winner and I would manage the kids, our finances, and the home. By choice, we were a one income family. My being at home gave him the freedom to build his resume and move forward in his career as a marketing director.

As a forty year old woman with only volunteer and limited experience in the work force, it was challenging to provide the stability needed for my family. Even though I got my real estate license four years prior to our divorce, I never sold any homes with it. I did not have to. It was one of the things I did with the hopes of helping to provide for the household in the future or something to do when the kids had grown up. My husband's salary more than supported our household so my need to bring in income was on the back burner. The day that I came out, I knew my financial situation was going to change overnight. I did not fully anticipate how challenging this would prove to be nor did I have any clue about the amount of time it would take. This quickly became my top priority.

The divorce triggered the instant need to decide how to fairly distribute the finances we accrued together. In my mind, "we" was actually "he" since he was the primary earner in our family. I know what he earned was technically "ours" but during that time I felt like a squatter. He did not impose this feeling on me at all, but I still felt like a freeloader. While I knew this wasn't an accurate assessment, I had a hard time not feeling that way. I felt awful this was happening to him. As a result, I made decisions without a clear head. Imagine how you would feel if you were in my shoes. I do not recommend making major financial decisions while in an emotionally vulnerable state. The forest fire that coming out sparked had not yet been contained. My husband and I had no business making the final decisions about how to divide our assets while the flames were still visible.

I have a relative who has shared pearls of wisdom with over the years. I was offered some very valuable advice about making decisions when in an emotional state.

Him: "Dawn, I am going to give you some advice I want you to think about."

Me: "Okay, hit me with it."

Him: "Never, no matter what, make any decisions when emotions are running high. Mad, sad, happy, it does not matter. Making a decision while in a highly emotional state never is a good idea. The results are usually not good."

Me: "Good to know, duly noted."

I have given this same advice to countless others, however in this circumstance, I blew it big time. Recalling this simple advice was difficult because it was buried under the growing shit pile and I ignored it when I really needed it the most. The crazy part was I actually thought I was in a calm and level headed state of mind at the time. I became annoyed when those around me suggested slowing the process down. I knew what I needed to do and would not listen to counsel from anyone. I was adamant I knew what I was doing and that everything would work out fine. I did everything to object short of stomping my feet and yelling "I do it myself" like I used to as a small child. What I wanted most was to have it all over with. It was that hard. I was convinced only when things were settled would I be able to get as far away from the turmoil as I could and begin my healing process. I would have made an excellent flamingo at the zoo because my head was not where it should have been. Thankfully, those who questioned the hasty way in which things were settled have spared me their lectures on how stubborn I am and the well-deserved "I told you so's." Chalk another one up to learning the lesson the hard way.

While we blew through the process, my ex was counseled often about not letting me take him for everything. He was encouraged to protect himself from his soon to be awful ex-wife. Aren't all ex-wives descendants of Eve, who listened to the snake in the Garden of Eden and subsequently unleashed all the ills of the world upon mankind? From where I sat, my biggest sin was not knowing I was gay until after 17 years of marriage. For those who not privy to the truth about my situation, my status changed from a devoted wife and mother to a deviant, lesbian, money grubber overnight. Perception is a powerful thing.

I made a conscious effort to be agreeable and fair, even to my own detriment. We divided our assets and I promised I would not touch his retirement even though I had none and was entitled to half. He got the home we built, the dog, and was on the hook for 10 years of alimony. Our divorce agreement provided for child support and temporary alimony. This amount combined did not cover the expenses of my new household. I got to keep my ultra- cool, seven year old, stinky minivan. Whoo hoo. We shared joint custody of our three boys. According to the agreement, we had equal nights with the boys in a month, however the actual time they were with me was greater because they came to my house everyday afterschool regardless of who had them at night. Out of practical necessity, we signed a lease for an overpriced house nearby my old house which he was required to cosign because I had no job or income of my own.

Even though we were no longer married, I was still connected to him financially. This made me angry and feel defeated. My choice to be honest about being gay was not easy. I endured the weeks after he was told and we were still living together. I took care of his emotional needs even though I was running on empty. My decision to come out and live authentically had given rise to more aggravation than peace at times. I made a concerted effort to carry myself in a mature and respectful way as this all happened.

Contributing to the difficulty was dealing with the kids' impression about the financial arrangement between their father and me. Despite being told numerous times they did not need to concern themselves with this, the boys still wanted some explanation about how things were working in the money department. One son in particular expressed he thought dad paying for everything for me was unfair. After all, I turned gay, left their dad, and, because I had moved out, he did not think it was right for his father to give me money. Fortunately, his father cleared this up by explaining how things work when people divorce who were married for a long time. In my son's mind, I was no better than a thief. This was a hard thing to digest. I felt bad enough about causing all of the unrest in everyone's lives and this was just one more nick in my skin that would need healing.

The turning point happened after one conversation with my son precipitated by a boogie board incident. I was in the garage of his dad's house and grabbed the boogie boards to take to the beach that weekend. The discussion went like this.

Him: "Did Dad say you could take that?"

Me: "Yes, Dad told me I could use whatever I needed."

Him: "You always do that!"

Me: "What?!"

Him: "You always steal stuff from him. You do it all the time."

Me: "Dad told me it was okay and I cannot believe you just said that."

We returned to the house and I was upset. He and I went our separate ways. I had been doing my best to give the kids space as they processed the situation and allowed them leeway when they expressed how they were feeling. Being called a thief were words that broke me. Until then I was very careful to not let the boys see me upset or crying. There was plenty of that and I felt like I needed to be strong for them while things were so new. I felt a conversation with this son was warranted, but only after the waves of hurt and anger passed. I needed him to know how hard this was for me. I was taking a risk and I hoped what I needed to say to him would conjure up at least some consideration for what I was going through.

Me: "I want you to know what you said hurt me. You accused me of stealing from Dad. You have shared your opinion you think it is crap that Dad is paying for everything. I get it. What I want you to think about for a minute is how this all has affected me. I did not just skip off and run happily away. This is hard. Really hard for you guys and for Dad and for me."

At this point, he stood silent and I started to cry. This was not something my children had seen me do very often.

Me: "I am asking for you to think about how hard this is for me. I left the house I lived in for years and left everything behind. I have had to do everything for myself. I have made sure you all were taken care of through this and I have been accused of things I have not done. Because I do not go off to a job everyday does not mean I do not add value to both of the households. I want you to think about that. Everything has changed for me. I just want you to know that."

I was seated on my bed and when I finished he walked over and just stared at me. He then lifted up his arms and motioned to me for a hug and shrugged his shoulders. He was never overly demonstrative when it came to showing affection, so the hug was his way of letting me know he genuinely heard what I said. This was a beautiful and honest moment we needed to have in order to move forward. What I told him was not meant to make him feel guilty or sorry for me. I wanted him to understand this was difficult for all of us and I was human.

When it became necessary to figure out a new plan for our housing, I felt like a beggar. Our rent was being raised and staying there would have been very bad for us financially. We looked into purchasing a home, but in order to do so we would need to use some money that had been put aside for college. My tax returns for the previous two years were anemic because of the divorce and I was required to put down 20% in order to obtain financing. I had to consult with my ex-husband before I used the funds for this purpose, even though the money was in my account. Fortunately we were able to replenish the account within a year of closing on the home.

Expressing or explaining the intrinsic value of someone to a household in non-monetary terms was not easy. Most women who have been through a divorce can understand this concept. For every woman lucky enough to have an ex-husband who pays child support and alimony, there is another who is not so lucky. Women who devoted their time and lives to supporting the family and delayed their careers can suddenly find themselves on their own financially. It is hard not to think about the possibilities and opportunities not taken when something like this happens. It is hard not to feel like a complete fool for not considering the impact these decisions might have in the future. I encourage you to understand that living life while constantly trying to prepare for the next disaster is not really living. I worked very diligently to fight the "waiting for the other shoe to drop" mentality after everything happened.

Around the three year mark, I felt I had hit a very good stride as I acclimated to the new look that life had taken on. I was growing more confident and comfortable as months went by and life began to look less like a battle field. My mantra each day was "things will be okay." I approached the task of renovating life with an optimism was not always shared by those around me. I spent most of my time being the cheerleader, which was a new role for me. My goal each day was to put one foot in front of the other and to deflect any negativity that came my way as this worked itself out. I began to feel momentum building with regard to finances and knew as long as I was getting financial support for the kids I still had time to continue working to improve our bottom line while my real estate career got off the ground. It only took one unexpected event to throw a wrench in the plan.

Out of the Blue

In June of 2014, my phone rang. It was my ex informing me he'd been laid off from his current six figure income job. He had no clue or warning it was coming. The wind left the sails of the ship I was sailing in route to financial independence. I could not breathe. The timeline I had outlined for when I would be able to provide for myself fully had shifted. Once again, we were operating in unknowns. I was not ready for this. I had hoped to have some time to build my resume, sell more homes, and implement the plan to provide financially for myself, my wife, and our children. Things do not happen overnight. I was determined to grow my real estate business to the point where I no longer needed child support or alimony. Women have long been accused of living off of their ex-husbands child support and alimony, but I was never one of those women. My goal always was to not need anything from him or anyone else financially. I lived on my parents' dime for the first 20 years of life, on my ex-husband's dime the next 20, and the final chapters will be on my own dime, as it should be.

My shock was compounded by the fact that within the four minute conversation he dropped the bomb that the changes in his finances might necessitate adjustments to our financial agreement. It was clear he was reacting to the sudden turn of events. There is nothing I would have welcomed more than to be able to share my sympathy for the sudden job loss and go about my day. Instead, I wished this unexpected development wasn't going to impact me in the immediate future. It was demoralizing sitting around waiting to hear what was going to happen next. I wondered and worried. How long would it take him to find a job? What were we all going to do? What if the new job did not pay as much? What was the impact of this new round of changes going to be? He ended up finding a job before his severance ran out, but many changes came as a result of this lay off for both of our households. In short order, I realized I had to move up in the batter's box and adjust to the curve balls that were coming my way.

While things continue to work themselves out, my wife and I find ourselves in a state of constant waiting. Wait to see who needs to sell or buy a home. Wait to see who is going to book a photography session. Wait to see when the legal papers arrive. Wait to see how the kids are going to react. Wait and see if being gay is going to affect the ability to provide for my family. I could go on for pages about the shit we have waited for. Our needs have been determined by what others have needed. The fact that we have been doing our best to raise our kids and keep the flow of life a positive one is important. The silver lining to this waiting game is we are receiving a first class education in the art of patience. We remain hopeful for what the future has in store for us as individuals and as a married couple.

My wife has joked from the beginning we should have run away. Some days I regret not considering this option. Some days the gypsy life looks pretty damn good. We have struggled on many fronts but we have fared pretty well as we continue balancing our businesses, raising our family, and dealing with the obstacles daily life presents outside this particular situation. Yes, our contacts and networking in our old circles is limited. Yes, our opportunities for employment may be limited due to the gaps in our resumes. The good news is we have chosen to move forward and rise above these challenges by creating a new circle of friends. We have surrounded ourselves with people who know and love us and do not have any prejudicial opinions regarding our past circumstances. We have mitigated the gaps in our resumes by working for ourselves and setting a path for success completely within our control. Our success is tied to how hard we are willing to work each day to get to our future goals. We have faith that God has everything worked out, even if we have no clue what the future may bring.

CHAPTER 11

God is Good

When I do good, I feel good. When I do bad,
I feel bad. That's my religion.

— *Abraham Lincoln*

Yes, I am going to talk about religion. Specifically, my personal experience. If you are curious about how someone can identify as a Christian and be gay then keep reading. If you are looking for a debate about gay theology, I suggest skipping this chapter because you will be disappointed. Faith is a uniquely personal thing for me.

My spiritual journey has run the gamut. I have been involved with a variety of churches, Protestant and Catholic alike, throughout my life. I have always had a deep sense of faith. By the time I graduated from college, I was only a few credits short of a religion minor. I was preoccupied with finding the meaning of my life and deepening my spiritual side for many years. This quest was my attempt to find Moby Dick.

I discovered many theologies have been created to accommodate and explain many aspects of life. Faith is belief. Doctrines are laws and rules put in place to guide the followers of a particular religion. If faith and doctrine had a baby, it would be named religion. In order to fully practice whichever religion you choose, your belief must be in alignment with doctrine.

Faith and religion have never been the same thing to me. It is possible to have faith without a religion. Religion is the structure under which a person chooses to exercise their faith. This may be simplistic but I think faith is the beach and religion is the vehicle you jumped in to get there. You can bike, drive, walk, fly, or skate. For every vehicle, there are multiple colors or styles to choose from. This may be an oversimplification, but you get the idea.

I was a cradle Catholic and received five of the seven sacraments the Church has in place. Before I came out, I spent a considerable amount of time reconciling my beliefs with the doctrine I was taught. I knew what the church teachings said about homosexuality and I always thought it was a bunch of crap. I tried every way possible align my faith within the confines of my religion but I still had questions. Remaining true to my faith while I questioned the theology and doctrine of the church was a challenge. A priest once told me the act of questioning faith or religion was one way God used to draw us closer to Him. Sounded good to me. The more questions I asked, the less answers I received. The answers to the questions I did receive did not placate me. This fact was freeing and binding at the same time.

I was a fully initiated member of the church when I was 13 years old. For years, I felt at home there. The structure and legalistic set up of the church was a perfect paring given my need for order and rules. I realized, however, in many ways I missed the point of it all until I was an adult. As a child, I found great comfort in the walls of the churches I attended and was involved with many ministries and groups. I would love to say this was because I felt I had a higher calling to be close to God. The truth of the matter was church related functions and activities were the only things that allowed me a furlough and got me out of the house without argument or questioning.

Most of my "churching" was done by friends or other family members. In my house, we were what are commonly referred to as "submarine Catholics." These are the Catholics who always emerge from the depths to attend Christmas and Easter Mass but are rarely seen on any other Sunday. When I went to college, I realized I had a very good understanding of how to be a Catholic, but no true understanding about what a relationship with God or Jesus looked like. Can you imagine that? After years of religious education, I really had no idea.

I attended a private university backed by the Southern Baptist Convention. This was the first time I was exposed to different faiths and belief systems. I took many religion classes. My understanding of the topics we studied broadened my worldview and caused me to question my own faith and how I practiced it. I quickly realized Catholics were in the minority at this university. I knew a handful of students who were Catholic and we were like fish fighting the current, swimming against a sea of Protestants.

In very short order, I was introduced to the idea of "being saved." Up until then, I was unaware that not knowing how to answer questions like "Is Jesus your Savior?" or "Have you accepted the Lord into your heart?" was problematic to a Protestant. I also found many differences existed with regard to my understanding of proper religious protocol. You mean people chose when to be baptized? What is this strange practice? Not all babies got dunked?

My working knowledge of what the Bible actually says wasn't strong because my learning its teachings occurred only within the confines of mass. In high school, I was shocked when I discovered the Missal was not the Bible. Two completely separate books! Once I became aware of the actual Bible, I never bothered to check it out on my own. I did not see the need. After all, the church knew what was best and I went right along with it.

Upon entering college, I was grateful I had cleared up the confusion with the holy book situation. That would have been embarrassing. While away at school, my understanding of God grew. I saw how others practiced their faith and it didn't look like anything I had ever seen before. I began realizing there were gaps between my faith and how I practiced it. I wondered if my spiritual life was lacking. I began attending Bible study with friends and for the first time saw how faith in practice looked. I saw God in a different way and started questioning the religion I had known my whole life. College was the first time I was away from home and I hit some bumps along the way as I made the adjustment. I found it coincidental my first exposure to the word of God happened as my wheels rolled over many of these potholes. Deep down I knew my faith was the only thing I had to cling to during those shaky times, even if my religion was not clear. I always had hope and knew if there was a way out of the mess He would be driving the tow truck.

I became more educated about historical facts, religious practices, and my own spirituality with every class I completed. My personal belief system developed and matured as my faith in God continued to strengthen. Writing papers was a normal part of the curriculum. In one class, we were asked to choose a religious topic with social implications. The sky was the limit. I chose a book by John J McNeil titled, "Taking a Chance on God." This book was written from a radical pro-homosexual viewpoint and discussed topics including the sin of homosexuality and the prevailing theory at the time in some fundamentalist circles that AIDS was a punishment for gays. The author presented a biblical case against the current belief that homosexuality was wrong. For the conclusion of the paper, I had to include a personal reaction to what I had read. The next part of the assignment was to share my paper with a fellow student who was a religion major and had plans to become a youth pastor. He was required to provide a written response. His response mirrored fundamental Christian theology. Homosexuality was wrong, but he personally did not agree with the arguments made by other theologians that AIDS was God's punishment for homosexuality. I then needed to write a final response to his comments. I could understand his position but did not agree with it regarding the sin of homosexuality as is presented in scripture. Side note: My paper received the highest grade in the class.

What possessed me to pick this topic? Good question. There were hundreds of books on a variety of topics I could have read. I chose a book about homosexuality. Hindsight. I have reread that paper many times in the last few years and am encouraged my position on this issue has remained unchanged throughout my life. I never saw the big deal. People love who they love. God is love. Where was the problem?

I was free to explore different ideological positions and gained a new appreciation about how faith and religion are defined. I realized I honestly did not understand the meaning of true salvation as it was taught to me within the Catholic framework. In the Catholic Church, there seemed to be more emphasis placed on following rules and traditions than there was on the idea of a personal relationship with God in His three forms. I did learn plenty, however, about how to feel guilty when I could never be perfect. There was always a thread of condemnation I felt when it came pleasing God. He had been a distant and scary entity to me for a very long time.

Super Summer

After my sophomore year of college, I landed a job working for the summer conference program at the university. I loved this job. I even had a pager, which back in the day was something that screamed I am important. I was on call day and night. Super Summer was the annual Southern Baptist Convention's youth retreat. A group of over 500 kids, leaders, and chaperones were spread out across the entire campus. The energy these kids brought was contagious and I was amazed by how much faith and spirit they had in them. A few times I caught myself wishing that I would have been in the same spiritual place that they were at their age. This was the first time I had a chance to be immersed in a full-fledged spirit filled atmosphere. I worked closely with their second-in-command and learned about the evangelizing that was taking place throughout the week.

He asked me many times "If you died, do you think you would go to Heaven?" and "why?" I knew that these were are questions that someone asks when they are trying to save your soul. Had I truly understood what happened when I received the sacrament of baptism, I could have answered affirmatively. Since I did not, the questions and conversations continued. I think I told him that I believed I was going to heaven because I was Catholic. I thought that I was quite evolved in matters of faith and spirit since I had taken a class or two. He explained that Jesus was the way to heaven and that all I had to do was pray to God and to accept Jesus as my savior. I thought I had done that.

It occurred to me that I had never been asked this question before and it became clear to me that I had never given the topic much consideration. I was Catholic. I thought I was all set. I knew who Jesus was, but I did not know Him. This threw me for a loop. Of course, this man did not leave out the very scary explanation about what was going to happen to those who were not saved when Jesus made his return. This kind of tactic may have worked on the kids that were attending the program, but I took it all with a grain of salt. My Catholic education had indoctrinated me with a full understanding of guilt, the fear of hell, and repentance. I was not scared, but I did begin to think about how limited my understanding of salvation was. I wondered how I had missed this very central understanding of God and why Jesus came to be.

I sought out my newly found friend and shared with him my readiness to pray with him. I know this is going to sound very odd, but when we prayed, I actually felt something change in me. I felt warm and an energy that was nothing like I had ever experienced before. This moment was huge. I decided for myself that I would live my life as a follower. I don't remember sleeping at all that hot summer night in June.

I was sure that this new commitment would make life so much more bearable. Once I came down from my getting saved high, I felt a little lost. I was not sure what I should do next. Should I go save others or memorize the

Bible? Perhaps travel on a mission trip to a third world country? I felt overwhelmed with the realization that I was a new Christian and I had absolutely no clue what to do. I had so much to learn and no idea about how to proceed. It was a commitment that left me feeling a little nervous. For the first time in my faith experience, I had no structure or traditions to follow telling me what my next move should be. I felt trapped by freedom. I was used to the familiar confines of my religion and changing course left me feeling like a city mouse that had moved to the country. I imagine this is how those who enter AA feel after attending their first meeting. What now?

My approach to life changed as a result of the experience I had that summer. Redefining my faith was easy. Figuring out how to practice this faith would be the challenge as the years went by. While in college, I was in search of something. I thought focusing on my spiritual being would provide all of the answers I was looking for. I would now be good to go with a peace filled life. Of all the things I regret, not knowing I was gay sooner is near the top of my list. When I figured out I was gay, I was angry at God for how long it took me to figure it out. Somehow it was His fault. I thought college would have been the perfect time for Him to reveal this to me. I thought if maybe I had been more in touch with who I was and spent less time trying to figure out how to fix all of the things I thought were wrong with me I would have gotten a clue. I was furious with the one unknown and possibly nonexistent person who, during my college years, may have opened the door to my knowing I was a lesbian. Seriously, I did. This thinking sounded sane to me until I shared it with my therapist one day and she almost fell off of the chair laughing.

Letting go of these thoughts was easy once my adult brain realized I was not supposed to know back then. God had other work to do with me before this lava flow could bubble up and activate the volcano. I went to college in the early 90's and at that time being openly gay was not commonplace. There were homosexuals, but homosexuality was not being shouted from the rooftops and certainly not from the top of the chapel at my Baptist University. It turned out many of the people I felt most comfortable being around were gay. I had no idea they were gay. Clearly my gaydar had not fully developed.

CHAPTER 12

Old Habits

Raise your glass if you are wrong in all the right ways.

— *Pink*

As you read this next chapter, please be aware I am just as confused about how I ended up fully immersed and back in the Catholic Church as anyone reading this may be. You are probably wondering what happened. Simply, we ended up going back by virtue of default. I became pregnant and that meant having to choose a religion for our child. This was a panic decision made primarily because we couldn't bear the thought of what happened to pagan babies. We would now be a family so we deferred to the familiar. We did what we knew. As cradle Catholics, we thought we could make being Catholic work because we had gained a better understanding of the church through our own personal revelations and newly gained understanding of salvation.

Our son was baptized before our marriage was made official in the church's record. This set the ball rolling. We fell back in to the comfortable routine of the mass. We knew what to do and decided to get more involved. I thought if I had a better understanding of the doctrine and tradition of the Church I would be able to seamlessly mesh together both sides of my faith experience. I wanted to become more familiar with the reasons why Catholics do what they do so I could experience the richness of the faith I had previously missed out on.

Over the course of the next ten years, I exceeded my goal of becoming involved. My children were small when I began my first ministries. I volunteered for Vacation Bible School and became the coordinator for the ministry of Mothers Sharing Program. I also landed on the Habitat for Humanity steering committee for the annual community project. While pregnant with my third son, I became a sponsor for someone going through the, Rite of Christian Initiation for Adults program, or RCIA. The RCIA program was in place for those who were not fully initiated Catholics and wanted to become a member of the Catholic Church. Every person seeking full initiation into the Church was required to have a sponsor who was a member of the faith. This experience gave me a VIP pass and the opportunity to receive detailed explanations of the doctrine of the Church. My oldest sons were also beginning their preparation for the sacrament of Holy Communion and as parents we were required to attend the parent classes for religious faith formation. This shed much light on why things were how they were in terms of tradition and offered the insight I was looking for.

I was trying to stay busy and continue working through the things I had going on in my personal life. I realized the more immersed I became the less I understood or agreed with. I became more selective with my volunteer commitments. When all was said and done, I had been a family life minister, coordinator for the MOMS program, a baptism prep facilitator, a purificator laundress (which are the white cloths used to wipe the wine chalice), head of the Mary Circle, a pre-cana facilitator, the altar server coordinator, and served on the parish liturgical committee. The more I learned the more I questioned and less connected I felt to God.

The highly legalistic structure and the focus on traditions took away from the spiritual aspect of my faith. I had attempted to create a cohesive plan for my faith that could flourish within the Catholic Church. I found out being behind the scenes and seeing Mickey Mouse with his head off was not helping things gel like I had hoped. I noticed many others were just as immersed in the inner workings as I was but did not seem to have any issues with practicing their faith fully. Time passed and I grew restless, wondering again what was wrong with me. Why was I having such a block in the faith area despite my best efforts to jump in full force? My anxiety level was growing despite the familiar structure of the church. As I understood more about myself, the less I felt connected to the church. The religion had once again created a block which interfered with my relationship to God. It was very frustrating. The more frustrated I became, the higher the wall between myself and God seemed. I wondered what I was doing wrong.

The truth was that I did not feel satisfied with the environment or the religion I had come back to. I felt like I had done everything I could to make it work. I drank the Kool-Aid and even gave some to my children. Now I was in the precarious position of searching again for an outlet for my faith journey. This began a few years before I realized I was a lesbian. In fact, when I did finally come out, I felt the block diminish. I felt closer to God than I had ever felt before.

I did not stop attending church immediately after I came out. In fact, I could actually sit in mass and hear what God was saying. I felt peace when I would listen to God's word. The rest of the mass was the problem. As my family struggled to deal with this change, we continued to attend as a family. It was not until I actually moved out of the house that I stopped going altogether. When I finally made the choice to leave the church, I did so free from guilt or any nagging feeling I was doing something wrong. I simply knew it was not a good fit for me. I have known many faith filled and Godly people who are Catholic. At one time, I envied their ability to live their Catholic faith with such certainty. For whatever reason, these individuals were strengthened by their ability to fully embrace the tradition and doctrine of this religion. I, however, found myself looking to downsize in the religion department.

As a woman who has spent many hours working within the boundaries of the Catholic Church, I observed time and again how women primarily provide much of the support for the daily operations. This was true at the parish and diocesan level. If you look under the hood of the car that is church, you will see an engine fueled by mostly women. Women seem to exist for the benefit of the priests. Like in a Broadway show, the stagehands were relegated to behind the curtain while the stars got to shine. This inequitable arrangement always bothered me. As a strong woman with sons to raise, I always try to impart on them my belief in equality of the sexes. This is simply not the true within the structure of Catholicism.

My personal theology is simple and includes my belief that living as a follower of Christ should not result in feeling defeated every day. It is a love based theology and hinges on the belief that I am loved because He fearfully and wonderfully made me. He loves me despite my multiple failings, flaws, and transgressions. In some instances, there is a big difference between what is preached and what is practiced in religion and churches. I believe God has no religion. He wants us to be in a relationship with Him and He uses what happens in our lives to draw us closer to Him. When an institution, such as the church, fails to consider the redemptive aspects of the faith then people have no hope or chance for making right any wrongs. Faith seems pointless if this is the model. Before I came out, I thoroughly researched the specific doctrine surrounding the church's position on homosexuality. I was not thrilled with it, not one bit. Based on what I read, I was beyond redemption. I believe the word used was "disordered." Basically, the very nature of one aspect of who I am will never be acceptable. According to this, where is my redemption?

Read what is written on Catholic.com:

> The modern arguments in favor of homosexuality have thus been insufficient to overcome the evidence that homosexual behavior is against divine and natural law, as the Bible and the Church, as well as the wider

circle of Jewish and Christian (not to mention Muslim) writers, have always held.

The Catholic Church thus teaches: "Basing itself on sacred Scripture, which presents homosexual acts as acts of grave depravity, tradition has always declared that homosexual acts are intrinsically disordered. They are contrary to the natural law. They close the sexual act to the gift of life. They do not proceed from a genuine affective and sexual complementarity. Under no circumstances can they be approved" (Catechism of the Catholic Church 2357).

However, the Church also acknowledges that "[homosexuality's] psychological genesis remains largely unexplained. . . . The number of men and women who have deep-seated homosexual tendencies is not negligible. This inclination, which is objectively disordered, constitutes for most of them a trial. They must be accepted with respect, compassion, and sensitivity. Every sign of unjust discrimination in their regard should be avoided. These persons are called to fulfill God's will in their lives and, if they are Christians, to unite to the sacrifice of the Lord's cross the difficulties that they may encounter from their condition.[1]

The Catechism of the Catholic Church states:

> *Homosexual persons are called to chastity. By the virtues of self-mastery that teach them inner freedom, at times by the support of disinterested friendship, by prayer and sacramental grace, they can and should gradually and resolutely approach Christian perfection [2].*

This doctrine is only one of the reasons why I no longer belong to the church. Although I am no longer affiliated, I still feel disappointed the

[1] http://www.catholic.com/tracts/homosexuality
[2] CCC 2357– 2359

---

church I was raised in, baptized my children in, and gave years of my life to believes acting on my sexual orientation is a choice. It may not condemn me for being homosexual and purport that having homosexual desires are not sinful in and of themselves, however, it does say that acting on them is. This is something I have a hard time making sense out of. When I examine that position, I cannot help but feel it denies the very sexual nature God himself gave us all. I just do not agree with it. I never have. The call to love is what I hold to. It may sound Polly Anna-ish but I believe love is the absence of fear. Those who fear frequently hate. I get it. Really I do. Those who choose to condemn how I live my life truly believe they are helping to stop the scourge of homosexuality from ruining the world. Unfortunately, those who engage in condemnation and hate often do so under the guise of Christian morals and beliefs. Sadly, if you are gay, dealing with fear and hate can be a daily activity.

It is hard to offer a satisfactory explanation for how I felt God was with me throughout my entire coming out process. Mentioning the words God and gay in the same sentence is a sure fire way to throw a match at a gas can. Of all the things I had to deal with when I came out, worrying about whether or not I was an abomination to the Lord didn't make the list. Many have a difficult time straying from what is taught in Sunday school and cannot accept homosexuality as God's will in any way, shape, manner, or form. How could I claim I am a Christian when the Bible makes it clear that lying with another man is sinful? Throwing Sodom and Gomorrah verses at me will not change my mind or make me feel condemned. Talking about how children cannot be naturally produced from a same sex relationship will not sway me either. I have three kids. I fulfilled my openness to the creation of life. Do I get credit for that part of my life or do I just get thrown out with the bath water because I realized my sexual orientation was homosexual? Again, where is the redemption?

"How can you say God is in all of it when you are gay?" For the hard core fundamentalists out there, this is blasphemous given what the Bible has to say about homosexuality. It's like saying I am an elephant and at the same time a whale. Fortunately, most who ask for clarification about how I can be both genuinely want to know how I am able to reconcile my faith with my sexual orientation. Of course, some are more interested in debating why the two are mutually exclusive of one another. When I share this with people, I can see their brain cramp as the "Huh?" expression flies across their face. My answer to the question is simple. God is love.

Hearing from any group or person about how sinful the homosexual lifestyle is in their opinion does not bolster their stand either with me. We all sin. At some point, I noticed when it came to being gay, the theory surrounding "sin is sin" went out the window. Somehow this trumped the rest of them. I found it interesting how the severity of sinfulness is often heavily weighted upon whether or not any physical contact or sex is involved, even for heterosexuals. It is the basis by which adultery is measured. Any act, thought, or behavior, whether physical or not, that distracts or is outside of the relationship between two committed people is an act of adultery. Acting upon those thoughts seems to be the litmus test. In simplest terms, or as the members of a certain Christian hate group would say, God hates fags. Those who take this position are out there and they represent the extreme end of the spectrum. There are also many good people who are not as vocal or obvious with their manner of protest, but they still do not accept homosexuality as God's Plan. They usually belong to the love the sinner, hate the sin school of thought.

My relationship with God is not dependent upon my belonging to a particular church. My past experiences with religion have been both good and bad. Since I left the Catholic Church I have found ways to feed my soul and grow my faith separate from organized religion. My break from Catholicism was inevitable and in progress well before I came out. My coming out did accelerate the process. There are those who believe if you are not a part of a church then you are a second class Christian and lost. I disagree. Those who suffer from this dangerously prejudicial mindset are the main source opposition gays and lesbians face when they are called to defend issues related to faith and morality. From where I sit, the roots of the hate tree often run directly beneath places of worship.

The Catholic Church with its doctrine and patriarchal nature just does not jive with my worldview. It is that simple. No judgments, no bashing, no regrets or condemnation. I understand now more than ever how essential it is to interact with people from a place of love. As my understanding of myself has continued to grow, I have discovered a passionate side eager to get out into the world and improve it in some small way. Every day is preparation for what the next day will bring.

CHAPTER 13

The Lifestyle

Kindness is the language which the deaf can hear and the blind can see.

— *Mark Twain*

I hate the phrase "The Lifestyle." The mere mention of the gay lifestyle conjures up images of half-naked people, over the top parades, and a rainbow colored free for all. It suggests living a care free and no holds barred life of exuberance and folly that looks like a night at Studio 54 back in the 70's. Everyday. All day long. For the past four years, I have been wondering how I missed this place. I cannot locate it on my GPS or on Google. Maybe we missed the UPS guy on the day he delivered it to our house. Or maybe it does not exist. Maybe it was invented by members of the traditional "lifestyle" who needed to find a less derogatory term to differentiate themselves from their non-traditional neighbors. We are waiting to get a notification in our email about when we can expect "The Lifestyle" to descend upon us.

We are two women raising kids and living a relatively ordinary life who have chosen to be with one another. We often laugh about having a "lifestyle" some don't agree with. We deal with the mundane and the ridiculous. We pay our bills, maintain our home, and tend to the myriad of daily tasks we all have. Our lives look exactly like every other family living on our block. How we live is very similar to the way we did before we came out. In the past four years, we have seen our fair share of trials and tribulations. We have dealt with the death of my wife's mother and gotten married. We have made mistakes and enjoyed some great victories. There is no difference between our lives and the lives of every person we meet. Through this experience we have become keenly aware of the lens through which we are viewed.

Frequently, we find ourselves fighting inaccurate perceptions despite the fact that our lives look very similar to everyone else's. Somehow our choices require more explanation simply because we are lesbians. Our marriage is a perfect illustration of this. Debating the morality, validity, and need for marriage equality is an ongoing talking point for us.

I never felt the need to defend my "lifestyle" or rationalize a life of debauchery because I turned lesbian. I offered nothing in the way of excuses or justification for my life as a gay woman. I was aware of what the Bible had to say about homosexuality. I also knew what the remaining messages were in that book. The rest of the rule book says I am fully justified in Christ because of what He had done for me, a forty year old divorced woman with three children who is in a committed relationship with another woman. Christ called us to love one another.

Consider this interesting fact:

> The Williams Institute at the UCLA School of Law, a sexual orientation law and public policy think tank, estimates that 9 million (about 3.8%) of Americans identify as gay, lesbian, bisexual or transgender (2011). The institute also found that bisexuals make up 1.8% of the population, while 1.7% are gay or lesbian. Transgender adults make up 0.3% of the population.[3]

[3] Gay Population Statistics in the United States. (n.d.). Retrieved from http://gaylife.about.com/od/comingout/a/population.htm

For a relatively small group, homosexuals are public enemy number one when it comes to their goal of converting unsuspecting individuals to the "lifestyle." It is hard to ignore the underlying sense of fear when religious based objections are tossed around like rag dolls. We are talking about people and not monsters here. There is not enough paper to print every instance of hate or condemnation those who identify as gay, lesbian, bi-sexual, transgender, or other come up against on a daily basis. The fear that the 3.8% of us gays will rise up and decide to improve our numbers is just plain idiotic.

Included in my reading was also the supposed "propaganda" seeking to convert children to the sinful "lifestyle." What?! I am unaware of any mandates in the nonexistent gay handbook that include instructions about recruiting children. This was and will always be the most ridiculous example of fear-based reasoning. When JCPenney hired Ellen DeGeneres as their spokesperson, a full on war ensued. Many loyal customers were shocked and unhappy about this partnership. What followed were heated debates on social media, petitions, and threats of boycotting the company due to the message choosing a lesbian was sending to the world. This kind of bigotry under the guise of protecting families and children pisses me off even though I know it is completely ridiculous. Fear based rhetoric and prejudice is something I scratch my head over each time I hear it. Fortunately, Ellen had the courage and strength to address the haters and JCPenney had the sense to remain committed to their decision. God casts out all fear.

Time after time, so called experts and religious leaders attest to the dangers we gays pose to the rest of society. Members of a certain Christian hate group run around waving signs proclaiming their version of truth which includes that God hates fags. They have a website and an agenda and I would love to know what God actually thinks about it. The only comfort I can find is in knowing we all will be judged by how we lived our lives, regardless of whatever religion we choose to identify with, if any at all. He will know our hearts. Defining people based on what they do and not who they are contradicts everything I know to be true about Christianity. Labeling and chastising discounts the whole person. The lack of tolerance for those who believe or think differently keeps me up on some nights.

Arguing with intolerant people is an exercise in futility. I knew this truth long before I knew I was a homosexual. It is not my place to convince people how to think or to judge them for what they think. The gift of persuasion was never in my wheelhouse. I don't get a rush from arguing and was never one get satisfaction from having to be right all the time. I am interested in fairness and justice for everyone. I learned early on engaging in debate will do little to change the minds of people who refuse to listen or consider my position. I prefer to remain focused on the overall goal of finding a way to reduce negativity and discord in order to find common ground. I would rather spend my energy teaching my children how to be tolerant of those who have different views and to be responsible for the choices they make in their lives.

My hope is at some point we can all arrive at a place of love when it comes to understanding one another. My optimism is the only thing helping mitigate the hurt I feel when I see and hear all of the hateful comments and protests about gays. Any sentence that starts with the word hate is suspect to me. The first word your brain hears tends to be what you remember. Regardless of our apparent differences, we are all human.

The messages from many pulpits state that God calls each of us to be who He made us to be, unless you are gay. Hating the sin and loving the sinner sounds nice but eerily similar to the "I love you anyway" declarations I heard in the early days. The truth, however, is most people are not evolved enough to hate the sin and love the sinner. We all sin. This would be a less offensive statement if we said it about every single person we ever came across. It is not. I have heard it used exclusively when referring to the sin homosexuals are afflicted with or better yet have chosen. Those who believe being gay is a choice have developed the opinion that being gay is greater than any other sin. Sin is sin. When was the last time you heard someone say hate the sin and love the sinner in response to an everyday situation? Think of the seven deadly sins. Have you ever heard someone use these terms when someone chose to be angry, greedy, gluttonous, or lusty? Hate the sin and love the sinner is judgment disguised as righteousness. We are not the sum of all our faults or failings, neither are we the sum of our victories or successes. I politely agree to disagree with those who think this way and move about my day.

Round and Round

I have always been a live and let live kind of gal. If I had to choose a party platform that best described my political views, it would be libertarian with a smattering of the green party. I am a registered independent because I like keeping my options open when voting day rolls around. When my wife and I married, I had the pleasure of speaking to someone who told me her lack of acknowledgement of the wedding was due to her religious opposition to my "lifestyle." This was a close family member. When I shared I was hurt by her silence about my wedding, I was told she would be going against her personal beliefs by offering a congratulations or any acknowledgement of the event. This would be a violation of her conscience. I was confused. How can someone else's actions violate another individual's conscience? Wouldn't it be a violation if they themselves decided to enter in to a gay marriage?

Taking a religious stand and being straight up dismissive are two very different things. It is ironic these harsh arguments are based upon a religion founded on the tenets of love for one another. I can say with confidence my conscience plays an enormous role in how I choose to live my life. If I steal from a store, I have violated my own conscience. For this to happen, I have to engage in an action, whether in thought or deed, that violates my own standards and beliefs. The only way this can happen is if I act in a way inconsistent with my own beliefs. It is impossible for what someone else does to violate my conscience. How is it possible for the things I do to result in someone else's conscience being violated?

I wanted to further challenge her reasoning. I tried to think of an example to better convey how silly this seemed to me. My children attend public school. This family member has chosen the home school. She does not believe in public schooling. The decision to home school was based on moral and religious grounds. I said to her, "Let's apply the same reasoning for your objection to my marriage to when your nephew graduates from a public school. It is safe to assume I can expect you will not be acknowledging his accomplishment or telling him congratulations?" She did not reply. I continued, "I assume because you do not believe in public schooling you do not plan to call him and say congratulations or send a card, right? Because you do not believe in public schooling."

She thought this was ridiculous. Of course, she said she would support him. I asked, "How is this any different from my wedding?" She did not have an answer. My wedding day meant so much to me. This violation of her conscience prevented her from being able to look past the circumstances and choose love for another person. I was hurt that it was more important for her to take a stand against my lifestyle than to be happy I was happy, regardless of whether or not she agreed with who I married or even that I should be able to marry.

Having strong religious beliefs is necessary for members of any faith or religious tradition, but disputes regarding these beliefs have placed wedges in relationships that are hard to pry loose. I have a hard time believing this is how God intended us to interact with one another. My dad was a product of a Catholic School education. He shared with my siblings and me some very wise words one of the nuns had expressed during his years in school. "I don't have to like you, but I have to love you." It is quite profound if you think about it. There has never been a more appropriate time to remember this.

Numerous states have passed "Religious Freedom Laws" claiming to preserve and protect religious freedom. These laws have suspiciously cropped up just as the push for equal rights has grown and the "gay lifestyle" has become front and center. Some offer protection for those whose religious beliefs are being denied because of the persecution homosexuals are engaging in regarding their practice of religion. In other words, these religious freedom laws make it legal for individuals to discriminate against homosexuals and anyone else who happens to be doing something they do not agree with. This is the world that we live in. Attempts to legalize discrimination crop up every day. I checked my calendar and it may as well say the year is 1950. "The homosexuals are squashing our religious freedom!" Every time I hear this, I simultaneously experience ringing in my ears and quite possibly a series of mini strokes.

The proponents of these laws are of the opinion that because they do not agree with who certain patrons choose to love they should be allowed to refuse service. They point to the First Amendment protections for free exercise of religion. As they see it, if they are not allowed to refuse service then their religious freedom has been violated. Maybe I missed something. The last time I checked hate was not constitutionally supported. I could be wrong, but I doubt it. One day I lost my mind. Instead of yelling at the television, I directed my response to the business owners asserting their right to freedom of religion by sitting down at my keyboard. I may have only been talking to myself, but what I verbally vomited summed up my frustrations at the time.

> *How many times do I need to say this? Am I missing something? Freedom of religion is your ability to practice whatever religion you wish, NOT the ability for you to tell others what they can or cannot do. I am sick of this. When someone says you cannot practice YOUR religion then your religious freedom is being impinged upon. Practicing is a verb. When a person comes into your store and wants you to make them a cake or serve them a meal you cannot claim your religious freedom is being squashed because they are gay. Period. Disagreement with a "lifestyle" or "choice" is an opinion and, while it may be rooted in religious beliefs, it*

is does not fit the criteria to be considered a violation of your religious free-dom. Baking a cake for a gay wedding is not affecting your ability to prac-tice your religion. If you operate under this theory, it may, however, greatly affect your ability to make a living, pay your mortgage, or send your chil-dren to Liberty University. Why is this so hard to understand? When you choose to say your religious freedom is being taken away and start pass-ing laws to this effect, it is goes beyond religious freedom suppression. It is called something completely different. It is called bigotry, hate, and dis-crimination. Practice whatever religion you choose, by all means person-ally practice that.

The way I see it, the only way freedom of religion was being denied was if those gay people marched in to the businesses, rounded up Christians while they were having a prayer service in the back room, and proceeded to beat them or burn their Bibles. As far as I know, there have been no reported incidents where gay patrons are demanding these religious free-dom fighters become gay. That sounds ridiculous, I know. This is my point. To them, being gay is a sin and not allowed. Super. So don't be gay. My homosexuality cannot violate your conscience unless you are living in the closet. And for the record, nor does my being a lesbian affect your religious freedoms. Do what you want, but allow me the same consideration.

CHAPTER 14

Rings and Pews

Where there is love, there is life.

— Mahatma Ghandi

When I was married to a man, I never gave it a second thought. We went to the courthouse, got a license, and got married. This was accepted and expected. When my wife and I decided we too wanted to get married, we faced obstacles not in place the first time around. My wife and I originally decided to have a commitment ceremony, but this seemed silly. We wanted to be legally married, but it was not possible in our state at the time. We instead considered doing something public for those who supported us. It was going to be a small gathering. Everything we went through to be with one another was sacred and worthy of a public celebration. Those who opposed were not invited. Our goal was never to convert anyone who did not accept our life or how we chose to live it. We planned to have a meaningful and intimate beachside commitment ceremony on January 18, 2014. We sent out save the date invitations. We bought lovely dresses and colorful sneakers. We picked a reception location. We were excited yet we both had nagging reservations because a commitment ceremony seemed to fall short of accurately conveying what we were entering in to. The deeper we got in to the planning, the more cliché it felt. It was becoming another wedding show only without the wedding part. We both were married once the "right" way and we wanted this to be different. We had already committed to one another and to be announced as life partners just felt weird. This presented a huge problem for us.

As the weeks passed, we tried to create something that would be special, different, and memorable for ourselves and our guests. We were uninterested in putting on a full blown extravaganza suitable for the pages of Bride magazine. Nor were we interested in having a raging gay rainbow circus either. Committing to one another was not a joke. It was important for the focus to be on our love and life together despite the fact that we are two women. This is what all couples who get married wish for on their commitment ceremony, um I mean wedding day. We are not cookie cutter kind of people. We tend to be a little crazy at times and this is something we are quite proud of. We love deciding and then un-deciding things. We envisioned a meaningful ceremony but not one full of all of the typical rituals and traditions.

Late one night, we made the decision to get married for real. In Rhode Island. On a random Monday. We wanted to be announced as wife and wife. Plane tickets. Done. Rental car. Done. Justice of the Peace. Done. Photographer. Done. In that moment, we stopped and listened to our hearts and felt such peace and excitement both at the same time. We were never more pleased to return the new sneakers and the lovely dresses.

The Waters Chicks have a unique approach to most things in life, but when we know, we both know for sure. It is never a declaration but rather a feeling and a subtle smile that seals our decisions. This is just how we operate. Ideas we begin with, never end up being the finished product. This is our process and it works beautifully more often than not. I believe the roundabout journey our decision making sometimes takes is for the express purpose of keeping our brains busy while our hearts are working out the details and listening for the truth to emerge. Our indecisiveness may be viewed by some as a character or relationship flaw or as an inefficient use of time. Crazy is probably a fair estimation as well. We consider the chaos in our process the gift of freedom to choose in any moment what we feel at our deepest core. In a strange way, it grounds us to one another and helps us to make the best choices in the end regardless of how large or small the decision may be. Our wedding was no exception.

Second Time Around

One morning, between answering emails and checking with banks about short sales, I realized in three short days I would be a married woman again. I was so excited. I sat as moments from the past flashed across my brain and could not find words to describe the joy I felt as we were about to embark on our greatest adventure yet. I would soon be married to my best friend. This day would be special, blessed, and such an important day for me. I was ready to make promises before God and the great state of Rhode Island to love no other for the rest of my life.

I was married once before and really believed it would be for a lifetime. I do not regret the fact that it wasn't. I choose to spend my mental energy considering what the future may hold, instead of dwelling on past details. I made my plan and God laughed. Fair enough. I quickly came to understand the path our lives take is not always ours to decide and God's plan will eventually be revealed when our hearts get on board with what He wants for us. All things work how they are supposed to when we choose to let love, peace, faith, and hope take up residence in our hearts and minds. My life had changed for the best when I understood how God made me and I was exactly where I was supposed to be at that moment.

After my moment of clarity ended, I went to check the mail. There was a letter from the Diocese of Orlando explaining my petition for the annulment of my marriage was affirmative. This was fancy church speak for it was granted. The process to annul a marriage can take months to complete and

I honestly had forgotten about it. Talk about timing. I chuckled when I read the very canonically worded letter and saw the grounds for annulment were the lack of "petitioner's ability to assume the essential obligation of marriage." I stopped for a moment and tried to think about what the essential obligations of marriage were. I thought I should pause and consider this because I was about to be married again. Having children? Check. Three to be exact. Loving and caring for your spouse? Check. Although my ex in laws would fervently disagree. But, I digress. According to the Church, I lacked the ability to assume blah, blah, blah.

A few years ago, this conclusion regarding my part in creating an invalid marriage would have wrecked me and punched my ticket on the crazy town express. When I petitioned for this annulment, I knew full well I was going to have to accept the fact that it was because of *my* past the marriage was not a valid one. I know now when I got married the first time it was not meant to be forever. According to the church, many things prevented this from being a valid, sacramental marriage. My being gay would end up being the cherry on top my annulment sundae. After the dust settled, I could see in hindsight I had become better equipped to deal with things not quite turning out how I had envisioned. I could teach the class on this topic at this point. The granting of my annulment did not make me question whether or not I was fit to be in another marriage. That was comparing apples to oranges. I had every confidence my same sex marriage to the most amazing and beautiful woman I have ever met was the marriage I was always intended to be in. She is my person. Actually, her being a woman has its perks. There would be no toilet seat disagreements in our future. Bonus.

Defining marriage is a hot issue these days. Same sex marriage is still a very polarizing topic within many circles. If you think the reaction some have about homosexuality in general is strong, just bring up gay marriage. I know those in my life who were silent or did not share in the excitement of our wedding are also on their own journey. I continue to offer prayers for understanding to those who do not view my love, life, or wedding as a valid, even if it is legal. As the wedding day approached, I had two secret desires. The first was for good weather. The second was, she would know without my ever having to speak a word, that she is loved, that I believe she hung the moon, and that she is the most cherished gift I had ever received. I also was grateful that we had the option to be legally married, even if it was not in our home state yet.

My best friend from childhood lives in Pennsylvania. She surprised me and showed up at the hotel in Rhode Island the night before our wedding. It was wonderful. One of the first things she told me was the story of her dad, aka my second dad, telling her 92 year old German grandmother about my wedding on their weekly trip to the grocery store. It went something like this.

F: "Do you remember Dawn?"

Oma: "Yes, I remember Dawn."

F: "She is getting married."

Oma: "Doesn't she have kids already?"

F: "Yes, but she got divorced and is getting married again. (Long pause) To a woman."

Oma: "A Vumon?"

F: "Yes."

I have known Oma my whole life and I could easily picture her as described, sitting in the passenger seat clutching her hand bag like the German version of Sophia from the Golden Girls. According to her dad, she just sat after the information was shared. He chuckled as he watched her eyes and brain try to make sense of what she had just heard. No other words were spoken. I spoke to him that night by phone and the conversation was short and sweet.

Him: "Are you happy?"

Me: "I am so happy."

Him: "Good. Some people are just not as evolved as others."

When I hung up the phone, I realized he was the first person in as long as I could remember who had asked me that question. It is a beautiful memory from that day that I still smile when I think about. My friend and I continued to catch up in the hotel room. An hour into the visit, she confessed she needed to come clean about something. Okay. I knew how this was going to go. I distinctly remembered she was never good at keeping secrets and 99% of the time we got snagged was due to her ratting us out. She told me her mother had made the trip with her and was in a hotel up the road. Apparently, she had strong feelings marriage was between a man and a woman, was opposed to gay marriage, and was not going to attend my wedding. She did not want my friend to tell me she was with her and had only made the trip to keep her company. She was concerned I would be offended by her disinterest in attending the ceremony.

After some prompting from my friend, I called her. She shared with me she had attended what she described as "a tacky wedding that took place in a swimming pool" between a straight couple. Before we got off the phone, I asked if she would at least look at the photos once we returned to see how happy we were and how beautiful the ceremony had been. I don't know if she did, but this was my attempt to change a heart, even if just a little. In her mind, the disapproval she felt toward the tacky pool wedding prevented her from attending mine. It went against her belief marriage was holy and not to be taken lightly. She also did not believe two women should marry. I respected her position, but disagreed with it. I was a little surprised at first, but quickly realized two things. First, she was not invited, so I had no reason to take offense to her not coming. Second, the reasons she chose not to attend were valid to her. These were her issues and had nothing to do with me personally. What mattered to me was my oldest friend had cared enough to travel many hours to be there for me on my wedding day.

Our wedding day was perfect but not without a few minor hitches. As our plane made its final approach, it flew directly over the city hall where we had intended to get married. Our jaws dropped. The historic building was draped in a giant orange tarp and the entire front was covered in scaffolding. It was undergoing renovations. We knew our plan to marry on the front steps was eighty sixed. On the morning of our wedding day, we made our way to the city hall to obtain our license and meet our photographer. After we completed our paperwork, we stepped out a side entrance and began to survey the surrounding area for a new space to have our ceremony.

Right next to the building was a garden right outside of the Museum of Art. It would be perfect. Our photographer arrived and we scanned the immediate area for potential places to take our photos. Directly behind the city hall was a little league field. I took it as a sign of good things to come. Our wedding party arrived shortly after our pictures were finished. Four people attended our wedding. My friend from childhood, another friend from high school who lived in a nearby city, and our hair stylist and his boyfriend who had only a few days earlier moved back to Rhode Island from Florida. The only person we knew would be there for sure was my friend from high school. The rest just worked out. We have video of our ceremony because one of the guys thought to record it on his phone; otherwise we had made no plans for video. It was an intimate ceremony and was exactly what we had hoped it would be.

The joy and beauty of the day is something I will never forget. I struggled for a good week to find the proper words to capture how that beautiful fall day felt. How could I adequately express how we felt like the only two people on the planet as we spoke our vows to one another? I was aware of how completely different this was from the first time I got married. I was struck by the expression of joy we saw in the face of the judge officiating our wedding, who was a complete stranger only moments before he joined us as wife and wife. I remember how my heart jumped when I saw her admiring the ring I had just put on her finger and realized we were officially Mrs. and Mrs. Waters. How could I put to words how much it meant that numerous strangers wished us heartfelt congratulations and best wishes for our future while going through TSA at the Rhode Island airport? Even a passing mail truck honked and flashed a thumbs up right before our ceremony started. It was a breath of fresh air. We could not get over how normal we felt while on our 24 hour adventure to New England.

We immediately went to the airport to begin our journey home. I was relieved our plane was one of the last flights to make it out of the airport ahead of an approaching storm front. We were on a tight timeline and did not want to miss our own reception because of the weather. This would have been bad and we would have had some explaining to do. As our plane made its final descent, a storm was moving out of the area. We looked out our window and saw a rainbow directly below us. Seriously, a rainbow. We landed, I changed my clothes in the parking garage, and we made our way to see our family and friends waiting for us at The Venue. When we walked through the door, I was brought to tears when I saw our sons' and the smiles on their faces. The entire room lit up. Teenage boys just do not smile like this, ever. My boys thought it was the best wedding reception they had ever been to and began calling it the "after party." It was so much fun. We swung for the fence on this adventure and knocked it out of the park.

A week passed and though I still felt like I could do back flips and smile forever, I had to admit I felt a slight uneasiness about how to share what we had just done with the world. Once again, I was in unchartered territory. How much sensitivity to others views or editing about our relationship would be necessary now that we were married? What photos should we share? Should we brace ourselves for people arguing about why our marriage is not seen on the same level as theirs? Whatever the reason, it was very upsetting and made me want to run screaming through the streets shouting at anyone who would listen. For as amazing and beautiful as the day was, there would be those who would never accept my marriage as legitimate. I have grown tired of being told I am loved "anyway" or having conversations that end with an "agree to disagree" position. I have been on both sides of this fence and the view is definitely not the same.

The view from the legally wedded side of the street does feel different and is special. When I look down the long road to equality, it is easy to get discouraged and upset. My unrest is cured by knowing in every moment of my day, I am blessed to be able to say I am legally married to the only woman who has ever had my heart, even if it meant travelling 1,044 miles to do so. For the record, while on our honeymoon, we proudly walked down the beach holding hands the entire time, horrifying many families and retirees equally. We did not care one bit as we were subject to double takes and stares, one of which came when we literally ran into my ex's brother who was vacationing near where we stayed. That was an awkward moment. Fortunately, it passed as quickly as it approached and we were able to enjoy the rest of our time with one another.

Pews

Another instance where our "lifestyle" became front and center was when my mother-in-law died rather unexpectedly. My mother-in-law was diagnosed with ovarian and colon cancer right after we were married. This was not the first go around with cancer for her. Five years prior, she had been diagnosed with colon cancer. She had surgery then and did not require any further treatment. We later found out from a friend of hers that for the past few years she had not kept up with her screenings. She was afraid to find out what might be happening. Her cancer was discovered because she was having gall bladder pain and the tests revealed the problem. She was hospitalized in November and never came home.

One round of chemo did nothing to help. In fact, it was probably at stage four long before she ever was diagnosed. For eight weeks, she was transferred between the hospital and the rehab center not improving and bed ridden. She needed a miracle, not rehab. The last few weeks were filled with emotional ups and downs, questions, and, quite honestly, some really good rants. After speaking with the doctor on a Monday, we knew she needed to be in hospice. I believe my wife was her angel that day. She was moved to the most wonderful hospice on the planet on a Thursday and died the following Tuesday.

She had worked as the Director of Faith Formation at the Catholic Church for years. She knew everyone. Her huge circle of friends were all people from the church, the very same church my wife and I had left shortly after coming out. On the night she arrived in hospice, there was a constant stream of people coming in and out to see her. This lasted for hours. We had become used to being the local token lesbians and continued to be undeterred in living authentic, open, and honest lives. We knew all of these people but did not have much contact with the majority of them since everything had happened. Our old world was colliding with the present one.

It was awkward sharing space with those we had not been around for a long time. Frankly, this was the last thing either of us concerned ourselves with. We were focused on what was going on in the hospice room. It felt like my mother-in-law was on display at an art gallery. There were so many people and all of the chaos became overwhelming for us both. For the most part, people tried their best to offer comfort and support to my wife, which she appreciated. From that point on, there was always someone in the room or in the kitchen of the care center.

On the third day, we needed to take care of a few things and grab something more substantial to eat than a bag of chips. As we made our way through the lobby, people were gathered in the main waiting area. As we passed by, a sweet older lady asked us if we wanted to get involved. We were not interested but thought it would be polite to ask what she was doing before we said no outright. She explained the group was creating teddy bears. Cute idea. The intention was to give these hand crafted stuffed animals to the children whose family members passed on. The materials used to make these items came from the clothes belonging to the family member who had just died. We declined and booked it out of there. We referred to these as "creepsakes." We know the group meant well, but no thanks. We needed a good laugh and got just that.

I believe when we are knee deep in sadness our brains go into a special mode. Laughter is the release valve that gets activated to help us cope with terrible situations. There were many moments when we found ourselves laughing during those awful five days. The laughter eased the sadness and helped us get through the process of watching someone die. Some of those times even included things that in the light of normal circumstances may have been considered slightly inappropriate. On Sunday night, my wife and I were in the hospice room alone with her mother. It was late and the channel on the television was parked on a very mellow music station. It offered us some peace and we thought it would be soothing to her as we were told she could hear everything even if she could not respond. At some point earlier in the day, someone had changed the channel to a closed caption news station and we wanted to find something else. We flipped through the channels and saw a Broadway show tunes channel. Mom loved that stuff. I walked away and sat down while there was a musical interlude playing. Before my ass could even hit the chair we heard a booming male voice sing "I Gotta lot of Livin' to Do" from *Bye Bye Birdie*. My wife yelled, "Noooo! Change it! Change it. Put it back on the other one!" I scrambled to get back to the soundscapes channel and half expected to look back and see her mom sitting up in the bed after the ruckus. She hated a ruckus. Laughing about this was the only choice we had.

Here is a more detailed explanation to those who are shaking their heads right now. At that point in time, we had taken turns telling her it was okay to go. The staff told us patients sometimes need to hear this in order to let go. We were afraid if she was ready to let go and heard the words to that song it would set her back in her letting go process. She was hanging in there and we racked our brains trying to figure out who the one person was she needed to hear from so that she could go home. I know, it is a little sick, but our wishes for it to be over were for her sake. Did I mention how horrifying it was? For however traumatized we were, we could not imagine what it must have felt like for her. That was the most upsetting thing. We jokingly begged the staff for some of the stuff they were giving her to make her comfortable. On Monday night, my sister-in-law decided to tell her to do what she needed to do, or not. Mom was not one who enjoyed being told what to do. It was really part of her charm. Apparently, this was what she needed to hear.

The following morning, our phone rang at 7:21 am. It was her nurse letting us know that we needed to come now. This was the death is imminent call. We had been on vigil and waiting for that call for 5 days and it still shook us when it actually came. We jumped in the car. I yelled at the slow person in front of us as I raced to get my wife to her mother's side. We arrived at 7:49am. The nurse told us she had passed at 7:45am. We were a little apprehensive about being there when she took her last breath. It was her final act of love and mercy in letting go before we arrived that mattered in the end.

The nurse explained she was not alone when she took her last breath and it was a beautiful moment. What we saw as we stepped into the room was completely unexpected. On day three, her sister had come from out of town to spend the weekend with her. She had encountered some issues with her luggage getting wet and had gone to the store to buy a cheap blanket to use while she stayed in the hospice room. She left the blanket on a chair when she headed back home. As we walked in the room, we all stopped in our tracks. The shock of seeing Mom after she had passed was fleeting. What we were met with was the image of Mom laying in the bed covered with that green and blue blanket. The blanket had a four foot bass fish on a hook placed perfectly so it looked like it was about to take a bite out of her hand. Seriously, I am not making this up. The nurse had carefully tucked her in and had laid cloth angels across her chest for each of us to take when we left. Mom was barely five feet tall and this visual is one we have yet to shake. Knowing her as I did, I know she would have thought that it was funny. My wife whispered to me the only fish her mother had ever caught was on a dinner plate at Red Lobster. The most profound thing I can offer to anyone reading this is simple. In the end, love is the only thing that matters. And laughter.

As a 42 year old woman, this was the first time in my life I had a front row view of the dying process for anyone, let alone a close family member. This was one hell of an indoctrination. To say watching someone die from cancer is horrifying is an understatement. Those five days felt like the longest days for my sister-in-law and us. We still struggle with being able to shake the sights, sounds, and smells of those long five days. We gained a true appreciation for how we all handle death differently. We took turns falling apart, laughing, and handling daily life while trying to keep some kind of normal for the kids as we were going back and forth to hospice. Our goal was to make Mom's last days comfortable and the hospice facility did just that.

Being gay does not change anything about having to go through the experience of someone dying. It just does not matter. We had a few moments of awkwardness before she died seeing everyone come through hospice. We had a few stares from nurses or priests who came to visit when I was introduced as her wife. When it came time for the funeral though, it definitely did matter. As I have gotten older and wiser, I have mellowed considerably. My confidence in this statement is the because during in the weeks right after she died, there were many occasions that warranted running, through whatever space I was in at the time, screaming with frustration, and I did not. To me, those were personal victories in self-control and adult maturity. I have much work to do, though, because each time I have resisted this temptation, my brain has been kicked into overdrive. This simply means I stew. My stewing process resolves itself usually through a series of small and at times humorous rants. Ranting is one of the many tools I utilize from the carefully constructed healthy mind tool box I have accumulated over the years.

Life for my wife and I has calmed considerably from the storm that blew through a few years ago. It seems normal and boring most days. Our normal was disrupted in many ways over those few weeks, however, some of the disruptions were simply nagging reminders of the fact that the world does not share our idea of normal at times. For the purposes of this book, what follows is a highly cleaned up and less ugly version of the actual rant my wife was subjected to. For this to truly make sense, some background is needed. I knew my mother-in-law before I met my wife. In fact, it was during her summer vacation Bible school program that my wife and I first met. My mother-in-law was included in our holiday celebrations and because of this my kids were very special to her. In her mind, they were more than her daughter's best friend's children, she considered them her grandchildren. My youngest son was especially close to her. They had their own thing and enjoyed busting each other's chops. She worried about them and always looked out for them, no matter what. We were her family long before my wife and I married one another.

We sat in the front row of the Catholic Church during the funeral, consoling our 10 year old who began to sob the moment he saw her picture next to the urn on the table in front of us. We all shared this experience and the emotions surrounding her death just as we all shared our lives with her. As the priest began to speak at the mass, he shared his condolences for her daughters, and my step-son. I admit, this was upsetting to me. My wife was upset, my sister-in-law was upset, and there were many who noticed the omission of myself and my kids. Seriously? I was not looking for any glory but I felt snubbed. We are not strangers to anyone at that church. We were previously longtime members. I don't think I really heard much of the homily because I was angry and sad at the same time.

In that moment, I was reminded that our marriage or relationship is dismissed or ignored rather than accepted or acknowledged by many. A good friend of mine once gave me a pearl of wisdom I often think about. She said, "You can't get chicken out of a can of tuna." I will give you time to think about that one. In our grief and the craziness, we forgot this. We forgot we are in the minority and that because we are practicing lesbians this particular religion's doctrine dictates we are disordered. The push for acceptance is the first step in achieving equality for each of us, regardless of our sexual orientation, race, gender, or age. Yes, there are those who are hesitant or unwilling to consider what equality means for homosexuals. Haters have been around since the beginning of time and will probably be running around with the roaches when a nuclear Armageddon or zombie apocalypse happens.

After the funeral, we went to the parish hall for a reception. I noticed my youngest deep in conversation with his big brother. I came up on them just in time to hear him ask my middle son where the coffin was during the funeral. I was curious to hear how he would reply. He told him there was no coffin and grandma was in the vase on the table. He paused and then asked, "How did they get her in there?" His big brother explained the concept of cremation and all was good. We had a good laugh and decided if she had been here to hear this she would have thought it was hilarious too. I am amazed by the things my kids think about and always get a kick out of seeing how life looks from their viewpoint.

It is important to remind ourselves during instances like this that the only thing that matters is how we feel about our family. How we are perceived by some does not have any impact on how we see ourselves or our amazing family. Stepping back into that church after everything that had happened was very difficult. This was the same place I was told to watch myself when I went to mass because people would be watching me. I was told I would be judged by those who were not in agreement with my decision to upend my family and take up a life of debauchery with my best friend. I was also strongly warned to beware of the impact my choice to live openly as gay woman would have on my children. Did I mention it was the priest who told me this? That conversation put the last nail in the coffin that was my membership at that church. Despite all of the negativity we felt, we were grateful for every person that day who offered us their genuine love and support because we were mothers, friends, and humans who happen to be homosexual. Included in this group would have been her mom. We knew this because we found our wedding picture proudly placed on her nightstand when we began the task of cleaning out her room.

CHAPTER 15

Memory Lane

Do not dwell in the past, do not dream of the future,
concentrate the mind on the present moment.

— *Buddha*

I had a sneaking suspicion many thought the two of us just skipped off into the sunset to start a new life. Life may have looked new but there were many things about life as it had been that remained. Coming out did not erase the memories of the past. Anyone who has experienced a divorce can attest to how difficult it can be to move forward while maneuvering around the emotional cones that pop up along the road to healing. Figuring out how to preserve the past memories while creating new ones was a tough task. When life changes it is natural to expect ghosts lingering in the strangest places. Holidays became a playground where the ghosts of the past played.

I have always found it difficult adjusting to change. I have yet to fall in love with warm weather during winter since I moved to Florida from Michigan 25 years ago. I do not like the weather in the sunshine state. I never have. I am met with disbelief when I share this fact. The truth is I like the cold and I like the change that comes with seasons. My inner child has refused to let go of the memories of how Christmas felt up north. Palm trees and flip flops will never replace snow and mittens. My dad broke his ankle on the first Christmas after my family moved to Florida. We were playing Frisbee in the front yard and he stepped back into a drainage ditch. It is funny to think about now, but at the time it was not funny at all. Well, that is not completely true. It was hilarious when I saw my mom run out of the house in a towel to find my dad lying in a ditch yelling obscenities. It was eighty something degrees outside and we were all in shorts and t-shirts. It seems unnatural to me to have hot weather to contend with during the holidays. Cold weather attire is much more conducive to the whole Eddie Bauer look I covet but have no practical use for as a Floridian.

When Christmas rolled around in 2013, we realized it would be the first time we decorated our new home. We had yet to create a décor plan and had not given any thought to where we were going to put things. I knew we would figure it out as we went along. If we needed new things, we would worry about it after the tree was up. I climbed the attic stairs in search of our holiday totes. I picked up one box in particular and was struck by how heavy it was. I did not recall packing such a heavy box the previous year. I set it on the ground and continued to remove the remaining green totes from the attic. I was distracted, still speculating about what the hell was in that stupid heavy box. I almost busted my ass falling down the attic stairs. After I brought all the boxes down safely, I dragged them into the house. Unpacking that heavy one was first on my list. I looked inside, got annoyed, and instantly felt a familiar shift in my mood. Crap. It was once again time to open the late in life lesbian's equivalent of Pandora's Box.

Even though Christmas was a special day for the two of us, we both noticed an increase in what I would call a "blah" mood surrounding the Christmas holiday each year. The house was oddly quiet as we decorated the tree. There was no music. The television was off and floating through the air was our quiet determination to get this done. We both hardly spoke to one another as we unpacked the boxes of lights and ornaments. This was our first Christmas in our newly purchased home and our first as a married couple.

We robotically threw things onto the tree. It seemed like we were racing to get it over with but it was taking forever just get the damn tree decorated.

After we finished, we sat and stared at what we had just done and then at one another. She asked, "Will this time of year ever get any easier?" I just shrugged my shoulders. A few minutes later I replied, "God, I hope so, because this sucks." We sat on the floor and attempted to nail down exactly why we were feeling this way. The answer came when we looked at the mess on the floor and up at the decorated tree. After some angry and sad tears, we knew what it was. Putting up the Christmas tree was like opening up a time capsule while driving 80 miles an hour in reverse. The barrage of memories was constant and caused simultaneous waves of joyful and bittersweet feelings for both of us. Seeing each of the kid's ornaments and reminders of how our families used to look was like watching our biographies before our eyes.

Although life was wonderful in the present, our old particular lives were no more. For her, it was a reminder her son chose to have very little interaction with her and to not to be a part of the Waters clan. It was also a reminder of the warp speed life passes and how in the blink of an eye their sweet baby faces turned into handsome young men. The memories are powerful and each year they sneak up on us both. We knew there would be emotional adjustments that would come as we dealt with the ghosts of Christmas past. We also knew that we would eventually create our own Christmas "feel." Yet here we were again, on that gray and warm Sunday in December, blindsided as these pesky emotions surfaced.

After some reminiscing and a few more tears, we came to a very important conclusion. Life was good. We knew the mornings of being awakened by pajama wearing bouncing toddlers were gone, but the days of sleeping in were here to stay. We knew our bank account didn't have our first million in it, but we knew we were blessed to have our own businesses and could be as successful as we chose to be. We knew life could bring ten day suspensions from school, surgeries, cancer, and fears, but these things weren't more powerful than love and peace. There are always trade-offs. The truth was that despite all of the perceived changes in the "feel" of things, one thing remained constant — our understanding of the true meaning of Christmas based in the love, joy, and peace God sent to the earth as an infant 2000 years ago.

Story Time

The "feel" of things is how our brains mark time and remembering those times help preserve our most precious memories. Even if there was a high likelihood of 80 degree weather, we could choose to be distracted from the peace of the present moment or choose to recall the blessings in our lives. Memories remind us of the story our lives have told. They are an important part of who we are. Stories are a part of our human experience. Every day, hundreds of stories are written. I am talking about more than just words. Our lives are moving stories. We are all stories in motion regardless of whether or not a single word is ever written down on paper. Life in action is the stringing together of every experience, emotion, and circumstance which in turn creates our own unique story.

When we are small, we are told fairy tales and nursery rhymes. I have been interested in storytelling my entire life. It came in especially handy when I needed to create a believable story when I was being interrogated by my parents after they had caught wind of something that I had done. Whether your tastes gravitate toward the real or the imagined is not important. Personally, I am a fan of non-fiction. This genre is the most interesting to me and helps exercise my critical thinking muscles more than anything else.

This concept was a fairly recent subject of contemplation for me. It occurred to me that our story is often very different from our personal history. Our stories consist of feelings, events, emotions, and beliefs that we have accumulated over time. Our story is really the reaction to how we see our life play out. For some, positive experiences allow for a very healthy translation of the world and result in self-confidence and a joyfulness of heart. For others, negative events or experiences cause a skewed view of life and self. Life can either be what happens to us or what we make happen for ourselves. Many of us have stories that are not based in fact, but rather in other people's opinions, actions, or failings.

Coming out was a make or break chapter in my story. Often we allow someone else to author our story and we are completely unaware that it is happening. Those who have suffered pain and hurt throughout their lives have a hard time healing when they are "stuck" in what they believe their story to be. One of the most powerful statements I have heard is that our "story" is what we cling to when we are afraid of our greatness. This fear is one that we all share. When we focus on what we have known to be true in the past, whether real or imagined, the fear of not knowing how to do anything else can cripple even the strongest of heart and will. For months before I came out, I was paralyzed by this fear. I had no idea how I was going to do this or what it was going to look like if I did. I had never known anything other than being straight. I was convinced that I would have to start a completely a new book altogether that was going to be written in Greek. It took me a long time to accept that my story was changing whether I liked it or not. I felt like I was standing on the edge of the Grand Canyon about to jump. When I realized that I was gay, I stepped off the ledge and away from all of the baggage I was carrying.

I began viewing my "story" as background information and the process as research and development that has brought me to where I am today. When I did this I was able to feel powerful and take the needed steps toward inner peace. Physical, emotional, and mental health is possible when our spirit is freed from the confines of our story. My goal was to be brave and willing to look at the facts so that I could once and for all, accept my own greatness. I did not feel greatness in me when I sat on my floor crying while I stared at my Christmas tree. Acknowledging your story is hard and the people that who struggle with this need the most prayer and compassion. Most of the people that we have seen exit our lives as a result of our lesbianism are stuck in their own story. I became determined that my past story would no longer be how I define my life. There were limited opportunities for growth or progress when I was gripped by the past. This is a game changer.

As I moved forward, I struggled with thinking that my life was divided in to three distinct time periods. Each time period represented its own book and I was a different character in each of them. It is a trilogy about Dawn. Book one was from birth to when I left my parent's house. Book two began when I married and ended when I came out. Book three began when I turned forty and is still being written. In order to feel contentment and peace, I had to recognize and embrace that my character in this story was not fractured, but evolving.

CHAPTER 16

Team Rainbow

Sunset is still my favorite color, and rainbow is second.

— *Mattie Stepanek*

As a family, we eagerly await the arrival of fall each year at our house. Yes, we celebrate the usual holidays and a return of cooler weather after the long hot summer. The excitement that swirls around the holidays pales in comparison to when hockey season starts. The arrival of hockey ranks higher than Christmas, Easter, and all of our birthdays combined. Our beloved teams are back on the ice after what seems like eons and we eagerly await the friendly rivalries that crop up within a divided house. Half of us are Detroit Red Wing fans and the other half are Tampa Bay Lightning fans.

We are serious about our loyalties to our teams and have gone to great measures to ensure our hockey newbie, aka my wife, was properly briefed, educated, and indoctrinated into our hockey fanatic family. She grew up in Florida so hockey was not exactly on her radar. Hockey fans are some of the most vocal and dedicated in the sports world. Body paint and pointy foam fingers are everywhere you look. She got a kick out of how crazy hockey fans could be when their teams were on the ice. She has become a Jimmy

Howard groupie and was a welcome addition to the Red Wing camp. Hockey opened up a new world for her.

Watching my wife become a full-fledged hockey fan was one of the fun and more exciting learning curves we have experienced in our family. The passion of hockey fans got me thinking about how many ways people choose to behave when they are expressing a passion and strong belief. Whether it is political, religious, or athletic in nature does not really matter. Passion is passion. Sports fans can be some of the most passionate people you will ever meet. When people are passionate about something, they tend to express it in ways sometimes considered annoying and obnoxious. To each their own.

Not only is October when hockey season starts up, but it is also when the Orlando Come Out with Pride celebration happens. This was a new blip on my radar. Is this a new holiday? Am I supposed to do something? What is this all about? With just over three years notched into our "lifestyle" belt, we still felt relatively clueless when it came to knowing what, if anything, we were supposed to do when these events rolled around. I support my hockey team because on a deep level Detroit and hockey is part of who I am. It is very similar to being gay. It is one part of me and I want to make sure I do my part to show my "pride" and support my new team. I spent a good deal of time thinking about how I was supposed to act or behave. It seems silly, I know. The reality was there were new things requiring my attention as I braved my new world. I may have just been drafted, but I was eager to get on the field and play my first game. I decided that the 2014 Come Out with Pride Day in Orlando would be the perfect time to make my major league Pride debut.

I was never a huge fan of gay pride celebrations and I say this with great risk of offending many people. My reasons are actually not what you would think. I don't like them because there are many who use these events as a way to further their anti-gay agendas. Gatherings like this are opportunities for those who are not members of or supportive of the gay community to confirm every negative stereotype that exists. Until this past year, I had never attended a parade or rally or gave much thought to going. I am a pretty low key person and not a fan of crowds or traffic. My wife is a full-fledged, card carrying member of the Norma Rae variety. When injustice abounds she happily becomes the "mad as hell and I am not going to take it anymore" crusader. She is passionate about her beliefs and in equality for everyone, on all fronts. She wears the activist hat in our family. I am less vocal in my approach to things that upset me. I write. I believe individuals should be allowed to express their passion when they feel moved to champion a cause. I hate injustice and inequality just as much as the next guy, but I usually take a more indirect approach to doing something about it. To each their own.

Behavior that is different or over the top sometimes does more harm than good because the message gets lost when the behavior is extreme. As a formerly straight, now lesbian, woman trying to find her way in the world, I feel conflicted when it comes to gay pride stuff. I appreciate being proud of who you are. What I have a huge problem with is being judged by most whose only exposure or opinion about homosexuals is based on what they see in a gay pride parade or on LOGO TV. For a multitude of reasons, it took me 40 years to feel proud of who I was. Discovering I was gay was one small part of my journey. I am bothered by the sheer numbers of close friends and family who told me and my wife when we came out that they did not agree with "the lifestyle." (Once again, I am still waiting for this "lifestyle.")

There were actually people who replied with comments like, "just don't go get a dyke haircut" or "tattoos" or "buy a motorcycle and wear biker boots." I am not joking. People said these things and much more. I have heard my fair share of flannel jokes and heard many terms I have yet to figure out the meaning of. Thank God for Google. These ideas and perceptions about what gay people do or don't do come about from assumptions based on the extremes. I resent when people view me with a prejudice about how I must live my life simply because I am gay. Assumptions and animosity are the evil cousins of prejudice and extremism.

Historically, the common perception about what gay pride events represent is not accurate. When you hear the words gay pride followed by festival or parade, I bet a picture of flamboyant, shirtless, buff men wearing thongs on a float comes into your head. If not that, definitely a rainbow waving group of rambunctious individuals pops into your head. For most people, this is often what "the lifestyle" looks like. Interesting. I can say the same image pops into my head when I think of a sporting event.

Shirtless, beer bellied straight men waving their team flags at a sporting event are never judged to be harmful or extreme or even viewed as obscene or inappropriate. It does not ruffle feathers in straight land because we all know as long as you are heterosexual all is acceptable. My being gay has not suddenly awakened the opinion I have regarding this particular example. This behavior is perfectly acceptable because when these painted, spirited folks return home to their wives it is assumed they will not show up to work the next day looking that way. Alternatively, I do not think most believe all straight men who paint their faces to support their teams and or attend championship parades represent a "lifestyle."

People who attend gay pride parades do not show up at work in parade attire unless they have a career in the performing arts. It was estimated over 150,000 people attended the 2014 Come Out with Pride event in Orlando. The parade itself did not look any different than a celebration for a team who had just won a championship. The parade was also one small part of the entire event. I wish there was a way to adequately explain this event to those who don't understand the "whole gay thing." It was very moving experience for me. The only word I can think of to describe the overall feel of the event was joy. It was everywhere, from everyone at every booth to each person walking around. The entire area was a judgment free zone (sorry Planet Fitness).

Being passionate about something is never a bad thing. The line is crossed when passion turns into hatred and an unwillingness to listen to those whose beliefs differ from their own. We all have experiences that shape our views and opinions. This is what makes us all so diverse and, on a good day, able to relate to those who don't share similar beliefs. To me, it's like we are all just running around stirring up shit for shit's sake. It is the quintessential us versus them taken to the extreme. There is no productivity to any of it. Getting a point across has lost all rules and decorum. The rallying cries of the left and the right are becoming louder and more vicious. Whether it is guns, God, or gays, things are getting out of hand. There are many issues that need addressing independent of our political, religious, or personal views.

Conflict for conflict's sake is unproductive and downright harmful to us all. The extremes are scary. We should all take note of what kind of fruit will be harvested from the branches if we continue behaving this way. Until we all step back and begin to act in a conciliatory and kind manner, the chatter and anger will only escalate. Our relationship with one another will improve when we reach the point where we can temper passion with understanding and respect.

I believe because we share space on this earth, what one does, we all do. We are connected because we are human beings. This is the truth no matter what your religious affiliation may be, what ethnicity you are, or who you happen to love. Behaving like the Hatfield and the McCoy's is not getting us any closer to the goal of understanding and respecting one another. We disagree for disagreement's sake and become more interested in the fight than in the outcome. We act like children fighting over a swing on the playground. We throw handfuls of sand in each other's eyes and laugh when we watch someone fall down and skin their knees. Yet, we mind our own business when see a bully knock down the weakest kid on the playground and steal their lollipop. We are turning into a nation of bullies and think this is okay. When did sticking up for one another turn into sticking it to one another?

My situation is unique because I have been up close and personal with ideologies from both sides. One of the most enduring qualities of the human spirit is the ability to see things from many sides and then decide what works personally. When some believe what is right for them is right for everyone else, tensions are heightened. We have become a bunch of hostile individuals intent on making sure no one is infringing on our personal freedom. When we stop looking for reasons to fight with each other and realize we are all free to live our lives as we choose then maybe things will improve.

Neutrality has become a rare commodity. Just turn on the television if you are not sure what I mean. Flip through the channels and I will bet my next commission check that you will come across two people debating opposing positions. Some are louder than others. Some even border on the ridiculous. The topic doesn't matter but the format is the same. I've concluded we are all walking around with our guards up ready to fight for something at any moment. Facebook has become a battleground even the most open minded and mellow among us are having a hard time understanding. It's a place where veiled threats and rants are commonplace. If it were not for my real estate and photography businesses I would delete my account immediately. The negativity is overwhelming and annoying. Are we all just that miserable and unhappy? Have we all lost the ability to engage with one another in a kind way? I hope not.

Adopting a policy of respect toward one another is the first step toward a more peaceful existence in a world where our values, differences, and beliefs are as varied as each human walking the earth. I am proud to say I when I was straight I was an ally. Coming out later in life has not changed how I feel when I see people acting foolish in public. As I see it, nothing good can come from engaging in heated and hurtful debates over beliefs or opinions. Agreeing to disagree has become a lost art.

CHAPTER 17

Broomsticks and Stones

That men do not learn very much from the lessons of history is the most important of all the lessons of history.

— *Aldous Huxley*

I have been called many things in my life. Some positive and some negative. I have never been a fan of stereotypes and am hesitant about making assessments of people based on them. Some days this is easier than others. I believe our default mode is judging books by their covers. I look at the person and make every effort to judge them based on who they are, not what they look like or what they've done.

Most of my closest friends could be classified as misfits. I was always drawn to those who did not fit into a stereotype. I never liked being stereotyped so I chose to avoid using them from a very early age. Tomboy. Jock. Rebel. Realtor. Gay. If you are like most, an image pops into mind when you read each of these words. Stereotypes are usually based on appearance, profession, ethnicity, or behavior. We rely on them to create an assessment of what we can expect from a person that is based on what we think we know of their type. People make judgments about others before a word is ever spoken. This is a dangerous short cut and can often be completely incorrect. I know I can be categorized in quite a few stereotypes. I mentioned a few of them above.

Tomboy. Rough and tumble and tough. Yes, it is true I loved dirt, trucks, climbing trees, slingshots, playing sports, and throwing rocks. If your understanding of me stopped at this point and was solely based on these few things, you'd have only a small indicator of who I was as a child. I also played with Barbie dolls. I wore dresses. I was even called sweet on a few occasions, which is usually not included in the tomboy stereotype.

Jock. Yes, I was a jock in high school. I played volleyball, basketball, and softball. I also had really good grades and spent my free time volunteering to help the elderly and sing in the church choir. These things are not necessarily the first thing you think about when you hear the work Jock.

Rebel. Does whatever they want to do and welcomes the opportunity to take a contrary position. Here, I am guilty. This was my college fun. I was never averse to seeing how far I could push limits. Yet, I was a Resident Advisor and taught in a school for mentally and physically challenged students. I also went to church every Sunday. Again, only a partial picture of me would have been painted if I was judged by this stereotype.

Realtor. Does an image of a pretentious, self-centered, arrogant, and high pressure sales person pop into your mind? At one time, this is what popped into my mind when I saw the glamour shot photos on the for sale signs in the neighborhood. Clients have shared with me their hesitation about working with a real estate agent because they have a certain impression of what real estate agents are like, which I discovered is usually based on how the agent looks. When they sit with me for a few minutes and see I am just a regular person who knows residential real estate, they almost seem shocked I am so much like them. The majority of my real estate peers are regular people who live much like our customers and are just trying to earn a living. Most of the agents I know are not anything like the stereotypical agent mentioned above. I suspect anyone in sales is stereotyped this way. Yes, there are some high powered agents exactly like my example, however, these are the exception rather than the rule. It is especially troubling to know that stereotypes are often based on such extremes.

Gay. This one is fun. Which kind are you speaking of? This is one of the few stereotypes subdivided into numerous classifications and groupings. According to my research, I came across a laundry list explaining the terminology for identifying gays and lesbians. I was floored. In order to accurately stereotype someone in the gay community, you really should spend a few minutes researching the choices online. I was shocked to discover that there are numerous subcategories for lesbians. For example, dyke, lipstick, butch, stud, femme, stem, which is a combination of stud and femme, boi, power dyke or even a hasbian, which is a lesbian who was a lesbian but dates men now. This is a short list. It's outlandish. Using the broad terms gay or lesbian only conveys information that these individuals are attracted to members of the same sex. For the life of me, I cannot decide which kind of lesbian I am. I did not realize I needed to diversify. Once again, I just do not fit into any single stereotype. It has also been brought to my attention there is a faction of lesbians who believe I am not a real lesbian because I was married to a man. I am a lesbian enigma I guess. Here is what I know. I can rock a dress just as well as I can a flannel shirt. I have long hair and have been known to wear a pink baseball cap backwards on those days when my hair is not cooperating. I throw like a boy but always cry when I hear certain versions of the Christmas carol, "Silent Night." I have high heels and black biker boots in my closet.

Who I am as a person has nothing to do with whatever classification I may be put under as a lesbian. It disturbs me there are those who decide things about who I am before I have ever spoken a word to them. This is one of the biggest obstacles we all face in our lives. This judgment was going on long before I came out but it certainly escalated once I identified my sexual orientation. I am my insides, my heart, my mind, and my spirit. Everyone is. I want to remind the world these things make us who we are. When I came out, I was told I was too hot to be a dyke. I was told by others they always knew I was a lesbian. I would have loved for someone to have clued me in a little earlier. But then again, had I known earlier I was gay this book probably would never have been written.

I felt the world was trying to redefine me after I came out. I completely understood this because I also was trying like hell to figure out what it all meant for me. Immediately it meant I was suddenly positioned as the authority on all subjects relating to the homosexual life. I let everyone with lesbian specific questions know I still had not been shown the secret handshake and I had limited knowledge of the subject. This was my first rodeo, yet I was still looked upon as resource for gay and lesbian information. My level of expertise in the subject was equal to those who were asking me the questions. I often explained I was still waiting for the official handbook to arrive in my mailbox along with the letter welcoming me to the club. It never came. I was figuring this out as I went along.

I became very amused by my sudden elevation to gay guru. I have been asked many times, usually by straight people, why lesbians want to be with women who look like men. Why not just go out with a guy? The best answer I have been able to give is because they ARE women. The preferences we have regarding the traits that make someone attractive are varied and unique to the person. Some women like big hairy men. Not this one, but it happens. Some men like women with curves, others like women who are short. There are an infinite number of preferences any person can have with regard to the qualities they find attractive in a mate. This rings true with all people regardless of their sexual orientation or gender identity. The best advice that I can offer to those who are looking for an explanation about what other people prefer is simple. Mind your own business. This mantra was one of the great pearls of wisdom I took away from the time I spent in Al Anon many years ago. Give it a shot, it really works.

Thug Lite

I was a typical kid. I liked to have fun and sometimes this fun was not something I would be pleased about if I found my kids were participating in the same. Growing up I lived in a neighborhood brimming with potential playmates. Through the years, I have kept in touch with many of the friends I grew up with. Most of my closest friends during my childhood were not what you would call popular. I was a misfit and drawn to others who did not necessarily fit into any molds. My best friend growing up was a girl who lived around the corner from me. We still laugh over the story of how our friendship came to be. I moved to a new city when I was in the third grade. I was "the new kid" trying to get established in my new neighborhood. While walking home from school one day, this blonde girl popped out from behind a mailbox and asked me if I wanted to be friends. She scared the crap out of me. After my heart rate went back down, I was thrilled someone was brave enough to approach the "new girl." I replied affirmatively and we have been friends ever since. She was my surprise wedding guest.

I spent just as much time at her house as I did my own. Her parents were like family to me. She and I were around one another so much there were plenty of opportunities for us to concoct the standard, and often dumb, kid antics. We thought we were so clever yet got snagged on numerous occasions. There was the super sly Speak and Spell caper. We figured out we could type curse words, hit a magic translate button, and this genius toy would produce the word in alpha code. We planned to use these words without fear of punishment that would come if we actually said the curse word. This worked for us until her dad found the notepad we had written all of them in. A phone call to my parents immediately followed. Grounded.

There was also the time we almost burnt down her house. We thought it would be fun to throw little pieces of tissue paper onto a fancy shaped candle in her room while her mom slept downstairs. At some point we wondered what bigger flames would look like and added some aerosol hairspray to the mix. We giggled like the school girls we were, oblivious that the entire second floor filling with thick white smoke. The fun stopped when the smoke alarms went off. I took off running and vaguely remember running past her mom as she yelled, "Fire! Fire!" or something to that effect.

Later that day, as I was laying low in my room, I saw my best friend walking up to my front door. She did not look happy. I knew what was coming. She was sent by her father to inform my parents of the incident. This was not a good day for either of us. Grounded again. I still have flashes of this day each time I see a can of Aqua Net. I was always game for a new adventure especially if mischief was involved. Thankfully, after the fire incident, our antics were less dangerous and more harmless. Our candle disaster made an impression for sure. As we got a bit older, we took our show out into the neighborhood. We soon discovered the joy of ordering pizzas for the neighbor across the road. We would sit in the window of her family room and watch the delivery driver go up to the door only to be told they had not ordered the food. This plan only worked because caller ID had not yet been invented.

What we lacked in creativity, we more than made up for in bravery. We lived near a huge Baptist church and had no problem figuring out ways to disrupt things by simply being on the property. See, we grew up Catholic and hanging out on Baptist turf was something that, while not a federal offense, was punishable by grounding. The Baptist church was a great place to play and we were not going to be denied the opportunity to exercise our growing bodies and our perceived right to do whatever we wanted to. One day, while her mom was at a meeting at the Catholic Church, it was mentioned someone had taken the previous Sunday's church bulletins and distributed them on the windshields of the cars parked in the Baptist church's parking lot during their service.

As I mentioned earlier in the book, the one ongoing problem with my best friend was directly related to her inability to clam up and be cool when things got hot. She just could not help herself and always ratted us out one way or another. She was a terrible liar and sadly I suffered many groundings as a result of her guilty conscience. She ended up moving away and I was forced to connect with some of the other kids running the mean streets of the suburbs. Back in the day, we had nicknames and labels for everyone we came across. Some were randomly generated and others were rightly earned. No one was immune from being labeled. I am sure I earned some labels of my own that weren't very kind given some of the shenanigans I had been party to. We used labels to communicate plans with one another without providing any details that could come back on us.

At the opposite end of the block was a family who was problematic for us. The mother living in this particular house could sniff out mischief from miles away. She was the mom who didn't hesitate to march right down to your house and give a detailed report to your parents whenever she saw something suspicious going down. She literally sat in her front window watching from a perch. As you can imagine, her children were not popular on the street and we had a strict policy of excluding them from any potentially shady activities. At times we avoided them all together.

There happened to be an alley behind the businesses on the main road we frequently cut through to get to our favorite corner store. That mother had eyes everywhere, including the back alley. If she saw you cutting through, she acted like we had committed a felony. We figured out if we got down on our hands and knees and crawled we could stay out of her sight-line and escape detection. We did not do this quietly however. We would make noises and chirping sounds to antagonize her as we did our thing. Not our finest moment, but we were 10.

My primary running buddies were a brother and sister team and we got along swimmingly. The brother was the funniest person I had ever met in my life and I was sure he was destined for comedy. This boy even won over all the parents when he really got his comedy act in full gear. This made him a comedic evil genius and our secret weapon. When the parents were laughing we knew they weren't wondering what we had been up to. It was a classic distraction technique and it was a sight to behold.

His sister was a couple years older than I was. She was the self-appointed ringleader and the bossy older sister I never had. The siblings had a swing set in their yard we made our headquarters. We devised many whispered plans while spending time at their house. I like to think we possessed super hero plotting abilities and were especially gifted in keeping our plans under our hats despite the fact their grandmother lived with them and had plenty of time to monitor us. As much as their grandmother had her eye on us, we sure managed to keep our hijinks under the radar. In fairness, she was a very cool lady and I am sure she was aware of much more than she ever relayed to their parents. She was a saint really.

She knew better than anyone that kids lack sense. Period. I learned this is true when I became a parent. I know I personally partook in nonsense and operated stupidly as a child and I have also seen these same things manifest themselves in my own children. This is not a negative statement, just an honest one backed by generations of supporting facts, anecdotal evidence, and science. This is the only way I can explain half of what we did as kids.

For example, there was a fence separating a block of homes from the Baptist church we used to cut through when we were up to no good. The last home on the block had a brick wall that went from the back of the home all the way to down to the street. This wall was wide enough to walk on. This is where "the man with the painted on hair" lived. For the record, this was the label we used and not a stereotype. His hair actually looked like it was painted on with shoe polish. We ascertained he was of foreign descent because of the difficulty we had understanding him when he yelled at us. Each time we would cut back through the fence, we made a point of checking to see if his car was in the driveway. If it was, it was go time. We walked on the top of his brick wall while singing Rolling Stones songs and making noises. He would run out of the house, broom in hand, and begin to swat at us as he yelled for us to "go away!"

For one entire summer, we bothered this poor old guy and had the bruised toes to show for it. Why? Because we were troublemakers. We earned that label. As a child you do not understand the harm silly pranks can cause. We were lucky no one was hurt or none of the neighbors were trigger happy. I realize with age comes wisdom and for most adults the follies of youth are no more than memories and good stories to tell at reunions.

With adult eyes I can see being annoying and inconsiderate just for fun was immature. Adults are just children who have matured past these momentary lapses of reason. Well, most adults. What I have taken away from these childhood memories in particular is there were better things I could have been doing than bothering people and being obnoxious. This is the case whether you are 6 or 60 years old. These events, while fun, were completely unnecessary and potentially harmful not only to me but to the subject of these pranks. When I look back I noticed our targets were often those who we saw as different from ourselves.

By virtue of being a lesbian, I am different from the majority of people I pass by on the street in any city or town. I became a target the day I came out to the world and spoke my truth. This switch has been the hardest for me to deal with. Our world is not a perfect one. It was not perfect before I came out. Now, the bigotry present in the world towards the gay community is something that personally affects me. I did not like the bigotry I saw towards gay persons when I was straight and I certainly do not like it now I am among the ranks. I am acutely aware of the reality that there are people out there who truly hate homosexuals. People who identify as gay have a legitimate fear of being harassed, bullied, or even assaulted in some way simply because they are homosexual. I am deeply saddened when I see or hear of instances of cruelty towards my gay brothers and sisters. There exist groups with the sole purpose of spreading hatred for gays. Many of these groups have also been responsible for the majority of the hate unleashed upon other minorities throughout history.

When we chose to run on that man's wall, we were not filled with hate, we were filled with stupidity and a lack of consideration. One of the things I feared the most when I came out was how I was going to be able to deal with those who hate gays. I feared what my kids were going to have to endure because I was gay. I wondered if their friends wouldn't want to come to the house or if their parents would have an issue with them coming to the home. Since my children were small, it has been drilled into them the most punishable offense in our home was bullying and being hateful. I like a good joke just as much as the next person, but what may be funny to some is nothing more than hate disguised as humor.

As much as I try to not let what other people say, write, or think bother me, there are times I feel deeply hurt by what I see and hear from those who are not gay friendly. It is not often, but when it does happen I am a mess. The other day I saw a photo depicting a wolf wearing a rainbow colored lamb suit. I was deeply hurt by this image. I get it. There are people who believe homosexuals are horrible people who want to attack the moral fabric of the world. For some reason, this particular picture sucked the life out of me. I have to guard against letting the hate penetrate too deeply in to my heart.

If left unchecked, it is too easy to cross the line from harmless fun to full on hate. For some, there is little to no chance they will change their opinions on homosexuality. For the vast majority of us, however, there is always a chance to change prejudicial thinking as long as we are open to considering the impact stereotypes and labels have on individuals and groups of people. Stereotypes, labels, and veiled humor are the gateway drugs to hate.

There is a two-pronged danger when it comes to making judgments based on only the few pieces of information we may have about a person at first glance. First, we unintentionally rob that person of the opportunity to open themselves up to us and be their authentic self. If we approach them with a predetermined assessment of who we think they are, we are creating an obstacle to connecting with them. Those who may not be secure in themselves may see this as a chance to keep hidden any parts they are not happy with or proud of. Second, we send the message that who they really are is not important to us. Approaching one another with open minds is the best way to prevent stereotypes from causing missed opportunities for interaction with many wonderful people. There is a great injustice when we do not have the opportunity to show someone we are more than whatever stereotype we may fall under. This allows others to assume fact not in evidence and to convict us of things not representative of our true selves.

Because of my efforts to resist the urge to stereotype, I have been fortunate to form some of my closest friendships to date. I am especially appreciative that since I have come out I have met many individuals who have chosen not to prejudge me based on my appearance, profession, and, most importantly, my sexual orientation. I have come across many interesting and unbelievably kind people I never would have met had I not come out. By necessity, I have ventured outside of my usual circles and been introduced to people and things I wouldn't have been exposed to before everything changed. In some ways my world shrank, but in other ways my world opened up. My wife is a photographer and an avid lover of the arts. She has dragged me to see some very brilliant performances and moving art work I previously wasn't interested in prior to our being together. I have learned that arts community is home to some of the most interesting, generous, loving, kind, and unique people on the planet.

My heart breaks each time I hear of a gay teen whose family disowns them after they come out. I cannot imagine what my life would have looked like had I come out when I was in my teens or if I discovered I was transgender. I believe had I known I was gay when I was a teen my parents would never have kicked me out or chosen to have nothing to do with me. This happens all the time. I have a special place in my heart for these kids and I respect their strength and ability to be authentic at such a young age. I realize times have changed so much for those who come out. My experience was a cakewalk compared to what those in previous decades have had to face. There is progress towards creating a more gay accepting society but still much work to be done.

I like to think I am doing my part in contributing to the goal of creating a more tolerant world. Challenging people to step outside of their comfort zones has been something I have always done. Sometimes this was in the form of busting balls and other times as a more thoughtful and calculated undertaking. In order to be who I was I had to step outside of my own comfort zone. There was no other option for me once I realized I was gay. As far as I was concerned, the issues people had with my sexuality was their problem.

One of my self-appointed causes is to be a living, breathing example refuting the ridiculous notion that those who are homosexual are somehow different from anyone else. Sexual orientation is one element of our whole person. I maintain who you choose to spend your life with does not fundamentally change anything about your core being. Coming out did not change who I was at my core. I am still stubborn, anal retentive, organized, mouthy, and always striving for peace in my life. My mind, body, and spirit all started working for me instead of against me and became aligned when I realized this about myself. Much of my struggle has come from these three aspects not being in sync. I cannot say the reason all of these things were out of kilter was because I was gay and did not realize it. Life is far too complicated to narrow down everything to one single point. To me, that would be like saying a road being closed in California is responsible for a traffic jam in New York City.

CHAPTER 18

Full Circle

The truth is you don't know what is going to happen tomorrow. Life is a crazy ride, and nothing is guaranteed.

— *Eminem*

I can count on three fingers the number of things that did not change when I came out. Paying taxes, my gender, and the number of kids I birthed. That is it. My sexual orientation changed from heterosexual to homosexual. I went from being a married woman to a divorced woman. I was a housewife who became a working mom. My status as a leader in church ministries switched to being the church pariah. My mind was anxious and then peaceful. My income shifted from stable to erratic. I saw changes in every area of my life within a number of weeks.

While it may have felt like my orbit was altered, the earth did not stop rotating nor did the sun stop rising or setting because I was experiencing this sudden shift in my world. When I came out I had more questions than answers. When would life feel normal again? How would my kids be affected by this? How would everyone be impacted by my revelation? One day, I realized all answers to my questions were found where I least expected them.

My back was really sore. As I tried to figure out what exactly I had done to myself, I started to laugh. This week in particular was a doozy and an education in dealing with the unexpected. I function best when my day has some semblance of order to it. Most days I plan and God laughs. Especially after my kids came along; most definitely when I came out. The days where order and control ruled were few and far between. I learned early on I had to adapt my thinking to allow for the fact that the only thing I could count on was I could control very little.

This terrified me. I began to live in a constant state of readiness just waiting for my day to blow up. I was hyper vigilant, anxious, and quite miserable. Unexpected events were my kryptonite. I believed if I did the pre worrying then when the bad things happened I would be better able to handle them. Not a great plan. Quickly I realized creating a mindset focused on waiting for the other shoe to drop robbed me of so much peace and joy. I missed out on the little things. When I focused on what could go wrong, I completely ignored the majority of moments when nothing went wrong. I also missed out on the many lessons just waiting to be discovered in the moments of chaos.

This brings me to why my back was sore. Earlier that week, our household unexpectedly lost a dearly beloved pet. Lightning was our rabbit for 6 years. She was very small when we added her to our family. Her name was chosen partially because as we were in the store buying her, a nasty storm raged outside. We were trapped in the store until the weather passed. She had a white line running from her forehead to the end of her nose. It was perfect. She also was our Mary Tyler Moore rabbit, she had spunk. Although I am not known to be an overly gushy pet owner, this girl did have my heart. When I moved out of my home, I left her behind because my rental did not allow pets. I missed her for the two years she was not with me. Once we bought our own home, she was back.

Seven months after she was back with us, I returned home from a flag football practice and was met at the door by my wife. She had the "something is wrong but I can't tell you in front of the kids" look on her face. She pointed to where the rabbit's crate usually sat in the living room. I was looking at an empty space. I immediately knew Lightning was gone. There had been no indication of anything being wrong. This was a shock and not what I had planned for the evening. We'd had our fair share of death and dying that year. My mother-in-law first, my mom's dog of 8 years on the day of my mother-in-law's funeral, and now this exactly one month later. We were all upset.

There is nothing more heartbreaking, and apparently back breaking, than having to initiate pet burial protocol. It was eight o clock at night, dark, and fifty eight degrees outside. Shovel? Check. Lantern? Crap. I had to call the neighbor and ask to borrow a lantern. All snotty nosed crying hands were on deck shortly thereafter. I started the digging after we voted to bury her under the tree in our backyard. I got half a hole dug and realized it needed to be wider. Boom- the shovel handle cracked. No dice on that burial spot. Lesson number one learned. Trees have huge roots near the trunk that will crack the handle of a shovel. We filled in the hole and moved farther away from the tree. Problem solved.

In between every shovel of dirt I dug out, we traded quips about how it was a good thing we didn't live up north or else the ground would be frozen. We laughed about how much I cursed as I hit rocks and more roots. We laughed when I threw dirt on one of their shoes because I could not see them. They should have been better at holding the lantern. Good times. I dug for about 20 minutes and got the hole to what I thought would be large enough for the box.

We ventured inside to get Lightning. The box we had chosen was not big enough. Lesson number two. Measure the rabbit before you put her in a box. I returned to the crate in our room and bent down to measure our poor rabbit. We then scoured the house for a box big enough to place her in. Lesson number three. Pet's dying on the day after trash pickup paired with semi-obsessive homeowners when it comes to having roach and silverfish bait (i.e. cardboard) lingering in the garage results in a shortage of empty, unused boxes. Eventually we found a box from my ski trip winter boots. This did the trick. The digging resumed to accommodate the new box size. We measured the hole and were set. Correction, we thought we were set.

I went to solemnly place the box in the hole and it would not fit. Really? Apparently, in our grief, we had overlooked lesson number four. A square box will not fit in a round hole. At this point, I was on my hands and knees using my bare hands to get this right and may or may not have been cursing again while everyone laughed at me. Finally, after more than an hour and a half of oscillating between comedy and tragedy, we placed her in her final resting spot. Thus, my sore back.

The oddest thing was, with each twinge of every muscle in my entire back, I was not really bothered by the pain. Instead, I was conscious of the sounds of sniffles and laughter from that night and of how precious the unexpected moments in life can be. Lesson number five. Be grateful for the unexpected things that often interrupt carefully planned days. I feel liberated from the fear of what can happen on any given day. The day I came out was the first day in my life where I surrendered to the unknown. That week we were all reminded the true meaning of life is found in family and the love we have for each other. It was time to say our final goodbye to our Lightning girl. It was tearful and beautiful. Lesson number six. Our family is amazing. I know my assessment is not an objective one, but I believe there is no better family on this planet. Lesson number seven. Eventually life will feel normal.

The previous month had been very difficult for us all. As a family we laughed together, cried together, and all the while were reminded of the love and kindness holding the five of us together no matter what life tossed our way. How we maneuvered through that month reminded me of how it was during those first few days after my truth became a reality for my family. We rallied together and survived the barrage of emotions that were hitting us all. We have all emerged from the unexpected changes that took place during the past few years magnificently. It was messy at times. For those who wondered and worried about how my coming out, marrying the love of my life, and living openly as lesbian would affect my kids, I offer this. We are absolutely fine. And unbelievably blessed. Over the past few years, we have weathered the storm and have grown closer as a family.

The fears rolling around in my head when everything changed did not come to pass. There were periods of adjustment that happened along the way and things that never even needed to be addressed. The chaos of the first few months after coming out has given way to an incredibly normal life. I am happy to report my kids are the poster children for the resilient kids' campaign. They handled the changes in their lives beautifully. Any questions I had regarding their reactions to their mother being gay have been answered in a resoundingly positive way. I learned nothing could change how they felt about me, not even the fact that I was a lesbian.

My boys are my biggest fans and I am grateful to have been entrusted with such fine young men to raise. They have each rallied to my defense during times they perceived I was being looked at with a sideways glance. They are fiercely loyal and for that I am the most grateful. My youngest is rather outspoken. (I am not sure who he gets this quality from. I am sure my parents could offer their input on this one.) He has returned home from school many times and shared with me how he told some kid off who made a negative comment about gay people. "Yeah, what's wrong with gay people?!" I am afraid to know what he would do if anyone was foolish enough to say something directly to him regarding his momma.

I am reminded of my sons' unconditional love with every little thing they say to me in passing as well as when I look at the school projects they have completed in the past few years. My middle son wrote an essay about gay marriage when he was in the eighth grade. My youngest just finished a social studies fair project about Harvey Milk. These were their ideas and I had no clue about the topics they chose until they were almost finished.

I shed tears while reading the dedication I found on a 6th grade language arts project my middle son completed only a year after everything shook loose:

> *I dedicate this book to my two moms, Dawn and Yvette Waters, whose encouragement throughout this project meant so much to me. Without them this project would have been started three weeks after the due date. Their patience and love is something I can always count on no matter what.*

I was deeply touched recently when my twelve year old informed me he chose me for a project about a monument in honor of someone important. When my oldest child was applying for colleges, he had to include an essay about a time in his life he had faced a challenge. He chose to write about his parents getting divorced. That I am gay was only mentioned in passing and I am sure was only included for the chance of getting some extra sympathy points with the admissions board. I have been overcome with joy when my boys begged me to coach their sports teams after I came out. Their insistence made me less concerned about what the other parents may think when they found out the chick coach had a wife. My concern was always to find a way to make sure their transition through this was as smooth as possible and this challenging blip of time would not alter who they were. They have risen to the challenge and exceeded any expectations I could have ever imagined. They are not the mushy Hallmark card types or the most touchy-feely kids ever to walk the earth. They are now all teenagers and have each found a way to make sure I, as well as everyone else they may come across, know how special I am to them, not because I am a lesbian, but because I am their mom.

As I look ahead to what the rest of my life holds, I do so with great hope and anticipation. There are still days where fear creeps in. I have to remind myself often love and fear cannot exist together. I am human and sometimes this process is quite ugly to watch but it is all a part of living. I am a work in progress. My mind is full of ideas and I search for creative ways to leave a mark on the world that will benefit everyone around me. As I continue to get a sense of who I am in light of the changes of the last few years, I will continue to do things that reinforce my authenticity. I have come a long way in my journey with regard to thinking I have to look a certain way or behave a certain way to be accepted. I have had the fortune of realizing the only person I need to consider in these matters is me and I am important because of He who made me. This freedom is priceless.

I am still me, but others now have an opportunity to judge me primarily by the fact that I am a lesbian. When I questioned the purpose of this late in life realization, I was so worried it would affect my kids in a negative way. This made me look at this reality in a negative way. Then it occurred to me this change just was what it was. I could look at it as a horrible life situation or I could put a positive spin on it. I have since decided I have been given the wonderful chance to help three amazing young men be more willing to judge people on character and not sexual orientation because of the fact that I am gay. This is only a small part of their own life story. The bigger goal and my prayer for them is that they understand the importance of being loving and kind. Working toward this goal may take a lifetime to accomplish, but is something that is worth the effort. I am a woman. I am a mother. I am a daughter. I am a sister. I am also a lesbian. This is who I am.

Not that long ago, one of my friends asked an interesting question. "If you had a crystal ball on the night before you came out, could see what the future was going to be like and everything that was going change, would you still have done it?" Without any hesitation I replied, "Absolutely." I explained the view in the crystal ball of what my life would have been like had I not decided this was more terrifying. Not being authentic was never an option. I would take everything and even more to be able to breathe freely and be where I am now. I would do it all over again. I am fully aware there are so many who have had worse to deal with when they came out. I consider myself lucky even though this revelation has been difficult. Change is hard regardless of the back story or specifics of the situation. As angry I was about how long it took me to figure this out, I am grateful I did figure it out. Switching teams mid game was not something I expected at the age of 40. I may have had to change uniforms, dugouts, and team mates, but I still was in the game. I plan on finishing strong and getting the win.

CPSIA information can be obtained at www.ICGtesting.com
Printed in the USA
BVOW02s0359180716

455390BV00005B/67/P

9 781457 543074